SPELLING BOOK

Words Most Needed
Plus Phonics
For Grades 1-6

by **Edward Fry, PhD.**
Professor Emeritus
Rutgers University

Laguna Beach
Educational Books
245 Grandview
Laguna Beach, CA 92651

FRANKLIN PIERCE COLLEGE
LIBRARY
RINDGE, N.H. 03461

D1262115

SPELLING BOOK:
Words Most Needed plus Phonics for Grades 1 - 6

Laguna Beach Educational Books
245 Grandview
Laguna Beach, CA 92651
Phone: 714 494-4225

Copyright © 1992
by Edward Fry
Printed in the United States of America
by Victor Graphics, Baltimore, MD
Edited by Reta Holmback
Typography by Käthe Sheldon
Art by Jeanne Cottraux Lynch

First Printing 1992

ISBN 0-87673-021-7

Limited reproduction is permitted.

Classroom teachers may reproduce enough copies of any Lesson for each student in their class.

College teachers or workshop leaders may reproduce any five (5) pages for teacher training purposes.

School Districts may not reproduce Lessons for distribution between schools.

Other than stated above, no part of this book may be reproduced or transmitted in any form or by any means, electronic or mechanical, including photocopying, recording or by any information storage and retrieval system, without written permission from the author, except for inclusion of brief quotations in a review.

****

INTRODUCTION

This book gives you the curriculum <u>content</u> of spelling lessons for grades 1 through 6. This same content can also be used for various special education, adult education, remedial and ESL classes.

The basic content of these lessons is the 3000 *Instant Word* list, a high frequency list refined and revised from the American Heritage study of 5 million words. To these 3000 *Instant Words* have been added 100 *Picture Nouns*, many phonograms and phonics principles, some content words from school subjects such as social studies, and variant forms of the Instant Words (such as plurals).

The lessons (pages) in this book are not "work sheets", though there may be times when a teacher may wish to duplicate a lesson to give to a class or an individual student as a "study sheet". This duplicated lesson may be used in school or taken home for home study or lessons with parent assistance.

Many teachers will also teach spelling using a less formalized curriculum content such as the words an individual student misspells in stories. Keeping a Personal Spelling list is encouraged -- see Appendix for suggestions. The lessons in this book may be viewed as a back-up or more structured and research-based spelling minimum.

Number of Lessons

Most teachers or tutors will think of a lesson as one week's work, but for some classes and some students, the progress may be slower or faster.

For grades 2 through 6 there are 35 lessons roughly corresponding to the 35 weeks in a school year. However, there are 20 lessons for grade 1 because first graders often start spelling lessons late in the year, or, if they start at the beginning of the year, they move at a slower pace.

Number of Words

The number of words taught in a first grade lesson is 10, in second grade 15, and in upper grades 20 words in each lesson.

The following table summarizes this information.

GRADE	WORDS PER LESSON	NUMBER OF LESSONS	TOTAL WORDS TAUGHT	LESSON NUMBERS
1	10	20	200	1 - 20
2	15	35	525	21 - 55
3	20	35	700	56 - 90
4	20	35	700	91 - 125
5	20	35	700	126 - 160
6	20	<u>35</u>	<u>700</u>	161 - 195
Totals		195	3525	

Laguna Beach Educational Books 245 Grandview, Laguna Beach, California 92651

Methods of Teaching Spelling

Since this book basically gives you the content, you must use your own methods to teach spelling. However, you might like a few suggestions based on experience and research:

1.   Use the Test-Study Method. For example, you might give a spelling test of the 20 words to all your fourth graders starting with Lesson 91 on Monday at the beginning of the school year.

2.   Have the students correct their own papers. Make sure they properly spell all the words they spelled incorrectly. During the first few weeks you should check their papers to see that they have both (1) found the words they misspelled, and (2) spelled them correctly. After a few weeks most students can do the self-correcting satisfactorily; however, there may be a few students who need frequent or continual supervision.

3.   Have the students carefully study the words that they missed, paying careful attention to just the incorrect or missing letters, perhaps by circling the incorrect letter(s) and writing the word correctly from memory several times. See *Parent Letter* in Appendix for homework suggestions. See also the *5 Step Study Method* at the end of this Introduction.

4.   Give a second spelling test on Wednesday. Every student who gets either 100% or perhaps 90% (your choice) will not have to take the test again on Friday. They can read or write stories.

5.   A final test should be given on Friday only for those students who did not do well on the Wednesday test. They should study again, just the words they missed and just the letter(s) they missed. You can help them by pointing out phonics, syllabification, spelling patterns, suffix principles or irregularities.

6.   Each student can keep a chart of final scores achieved on their final spelling test (Wednesday or Friday). See Chart in Appendix 12.

Supplemental Parts of the Lessons

Phrases and Sentences. Each lesson for grades 1 and 2 (Lessons 1 through 55) have some phrases and sentences which use the spelling words in that lesson in context. These are just to give a little practice reading these words in context, which will add a bit of meaning. Some teachers may use these phrases and sentences as part of reading or handwriting lessons. There are no phrases and sentences beyond Lesson 55.

Word Study. Each lesson has a Word Study part which is often a phonogram family (make, lake, take, etc.), and some comment on one of the spelling words. The phonogram is taken from one of the spelling words. You can use this section for teaching about words and word patterns. In Grade 3 and above, more morphemes (like prefixes and suffixes) and other word patterns are introduced. Upper grade Word Study often makes interesting comments about word origins.

Phonics. All lessons for Grades 1 and 2 have phonics lessons that illustrate a common phoneme-grapheme correspondence. Most of the major phonics principles are covered. See the chart in Appendix 7 for an index to phonic skills taught lesson by lesson. Since the phonics correspondence in each lesson is based on one or more words in the lesson, this further explains the phonetic basis for English spelling. Of course, if you don't like to teach phonics, you can skip this part of the lesson. The Preface which follows contains a discussion of phonics versus the whole word position in selecting spelling words and Appendix 8 has a rather complete set of phonics principles in useful chart form.

Variant Forms. In all lessons above Grade 2, variant forms of the 20 basic spelling lesson words (the *Instant Words*) are given. For example, the variant form for the base word "copy" are "copied, copies, copying". Some teachers may wish to teach these variant forms and some may not. This is also a way of differentiating lessons between good spellers and slow spellers. The better students get more variant forms. The most common form of the word is the one in the basic spelling lesson, even though it might be the plural form or the past tense form.

Personal Spelling List. Each student can keep his or her own Personal Spelling List. On this list might be words missed on a final spelling test and words that the student has asked for, had to look up or spelled incorrectly during story writing. This list can be used for personal study, reference when writing future stories, and supplemental games and drills. See Appendix 5 for more suggestions.

Review. Some review definitely helps the permanence of learning anything. At the bottom of each lesson page there is a suggested review schedule. This schedule is based on a 4 week cycle. Every 4th week a review of selected main spelling words is suggested, on the next week a review of Word Study in the preceding 4 lessons is suggested, on the next week a review of the preceding 4 weeks of Phonics sections is suggested, and on the 7th week the teacher can check to see if each student is keeping up a Personal Spelling List. These review suggestions given with each lesson can also help the teacher in formulating weekly lesson plans.

General Comments About Spelling Teaching

- Most spelling experts agree that good pronunciation helps learning to spell. Exaggerate enunciation when giving the spelling words. Some teachers introduce the words by pronouncing them syllable by syllable. You may have noticed that often National Spelling Bee champions do that.

- Point out trouble parts of words like silent letters or unusual or non-phonetic parts of words.

- Point out regular rules and regular phonic principles in words.

- Discuss meaning and use of each word. Use the word in a sentence when giving the spelling test.

- Vowels cause more trouble than consonants. Stress vowel sounds and the way they are spelled.

- Give students a lot of praise for good spelling, particularly if they are showing improvement. Look at their Spelling Progress Charts regularly.

- Don't let spelling get in the way of good story writing. Let students use invented spelling on first drafts. Later they can proofread and correct.

- Have a little fun. Play some spelling games like Scrabble® or have a spelling bee. Laugh at some mistakes, both theirs and yours. Remember that the only people who don't make spelling errors are people who don't write anything.

- For most writers, a relatively <u>few words account for a large percentage of their spelling errors.</u> This weakness can be helped by keeping a personal list of words often misspelled.

- Many students are helped by <u>emphasizing a visual approach.</u> Have them stop and look very carefully at corrected spellings.

- <u>A remedial method</u> used by many classroom and special education teachers is the kinesthetic approach. In this method a student traces a large version of the word with a finger while saying the word syllable by syllable. Next the student writes the word without looking at the sample. This is also used by some primary teachers.

- <u>Reference works</u> help every writer. Nearly every computer word-processing program has a spelling checker; students have long been told to "look it up in the dictionary"; and most secretaries and writers have a "word book", which is simply a big list of words (without definitions so it is faster to find the word than in a dictionary). There are also simple "word books" for students and, if you are rich, small electronic spelling checkers (student types in the word and the device either says it is correct or gives some possible correct spellings).

- Don't forget to give some occasional lessons on <u>dictionary use.</u> Good school dictionaries usually have helpful suggestions in their introduction. Knowing the amount of phonics covered in the first 55 lessons of this book will definitely help you in teaching any dictionary pronunciation system.

- <u>Memory Devices</u> (mnemonics) sometimes help students to remember difficult parts of words. For example, "Is there one 'n' or two 'n's' in 'annual'?" A memory device is that Ann's name is at the beginning. Another memory device is that Al is in the navy, so "naval" has "al" at the end. "Nav<u>e</u>l" means something in the middle of his belly. Note that "arc" ends in "c", which is like the part of a circle; the other "ark" is a boat for biblical animals. See Appendix 14 for more memory devices (mnemonics).

5 Step Word Study Method For Students

1. <u>Look</u> at the whole word carefully.

2. <u>Say</u> the word aloud to yourself.

3. <u>Spell</u> say each letter to yourself.

4. <u>Write</u> the word from memory
    (cover word and write it)

5. <u>Check</u> your written word against the correct spelling
    (circle errors and repeat Steps 4 & 5).

PREFACE OR SPELLING ESSAY

It is scientifically proven that English spelling is a mess. According to Dewey (1971), who did a major study of spelling, there are 145 ways to spell 24 consonant sounds. And vowels are even worse with 216 ways to spell 17 vowel sounds.

It is a flat out miracle that anybody learns to spell anything.

Yet, they do. You can observe preschoolers and kindergardeners use "invented spelling" to begin to approximate correct written language. They spell "love" as "luv" without being taught any spelling or much about writing.

This shows that they have internalized some elemental phonics rules. Invented spelling is not limited to preschoolers either. We see it all through the school years and even into quite mature adulthood. In fact, almost everybody uses some invented spelling at one time or another.

Most invented spelling follows some logical rules. The child who spells cat as "kat" or nose as "noz" has surely mastered some basic elements of language; or if you wish to be more learned, the child has mastered some of the regularity of phoneme-grapheme relationships.

However, the child who writes "luv" hasn't mastered enough "rules" or else he has not mastered enough "exceptions" for correct spelling. Hence, one of the major problems in learning to spell or in teaching spelling is "How many rules do you need to learn to spell everything correctly?", or "How many basic rules do you need and how many exceptions do you need?", or "Should everything be treated as an exception and you simply learn to spell every word as if it is unique (no rules)?"

Research can give us some answers.

The Hanna (1966) study taught a computer a great many rules (an algorithm) that had 3,130 rules (which included phonics). That is probably a lot more than you ever expected and a lot more than you could ever memorize. Using this large amount of rules, the computer, when given the correct pronunciation (phonemes), was able to spell about 50% of a 17,000 word vocabulary correctly. Now a glass that is half full is also half empty. It is pretty good that the computer could spell half the words correctly. But, on the other hand, most teachers or businessmen would not accept a letter that had 50% of the words spelled wrong. So rules alone cannot be an acceptable spelling program.

Another important line of research has been word frequency studies (The American Herritage list by Carroll (1971) and Thorndike and Lorge (1944) list), which have shown that a small number of words make up a large percentage of all writing. For example, a modification of the Carroll list by Sakiey and Fry [this author] (1984) showed that only 300 high frequency words (the first few *Instant Words*) make up 65% of all written material. Unfortunately, however, you can't just add a few more words and get to 100%.

Approximately 1,000 *Instant Words* make up 90%, but from there on it gets worse. How bad? Well, if we look at the Carroll research, we can see that in counting 5 million running words, they found about 87,000 different words. Of these 87,000 different words, almost half occurred only once in the 5 million running words. A running word is simply the total word count of an article - the word "the" appeared many times and each time it is included in the running word count. Research shows that, while we mostly use just a few words, there are a lot of words that we simply do not use very often at all.

Rules and phonic regularity knowledge will help us to learn to spell many of those 87,000 words, but certainly not all of them.

Therefore, the plan of this book is to try to take advantage of both of these important kinds of language research. It makes sense to teach the highest frequency words because these are the words that everybody uses most in writing: words like "the" and "is" and "boy". Incidentally, some of the highest frequency words have the most obscure "rules", if they have any at all. A common word like "of" might more regularly be spelled "uv" and a word like "woman" might be spelled "wuman", given regular phonic rules.

On the other hand, it is impossible to ignore the observations from the invented spelling of beginning writers and the high degree of regularity for some spelling patterns. For example, if you know some beginning consonant spellings and the phonogram "at", you don't have much trouble learning to spell "hat, bat, sat, rat or mat". Common observation and Hanna's 50% are important.

So the basic plan of this Speller is to teach a 3,000 word high frequency vocabulary plus some subject words, and augment them with "Word Study", which will include (1) phonics rules and phonograms, (2) morphemes like prefixes and suffixes, and (3) comments on grammar and spelling rules.

However, when you get down to specific lessons for actual children, you start to run into problems and have to make many decisions. For example, the first hundred *Instant Words*, our high frequency list, contains mostly structure words like "the, this, of". While they occur all the time (in fact, you can't write without them), you also can't write without some subject words. Hence, I have added a hundred *Picture Nouns* to the first 20 lessons, which are approximately the first grade level of lessons. Now the beginning writer can actually write a lot of meaningful sentences and stories very early in the "learning to write and spell lesson" sequence.

I strongly encourage a lot of writing. It is a valuable and necessary communication skill. It's the output half of "literacy", and modern society demands literacy for all of its successful and effective members. I also subscribe to the idea that it is important to write a rough draft, spelling any way you can, then clean it up. But, as any writer matures, his or her "rough draft" has more mature spelling and less cleaning up is required. Or at least the cleaning up of common words is not required. It is one thing not to know how to spell "pneumonia" and another thing not to know how to spell "their". You are simply not literate if you don't know how to spell most common words and any teacher in any subject, or any employer, or any good friend receiving your letter will tell you so. Invented spelling is OK for kids or newly literate adults, but with maturity it has to go.

This Spelling Book is dedicated to the proposition that every elementary teacher should have regular weekly spelling lessons. I am all in favor of teachers correcting students' written stories and having the pupils study their mistakes. From these mistakes the pupil can keep a "Personal Spelling List", which is a valuable learning to spell technique. But I am also in favor of teachers holding systematic spelling lessons that cover the two spelling fundamentals: (1) high frequency words, and (2) some rules (which include phonics).

We have talked about two important aspects of educational research concerning word frequency counts and spelling rules. There is yet another aspect of educational research that has important bearing and that is the "learning how" to spell research. It has several important things to say. The first is that you should follow a test-study-test sequence, not a study-test sequence. What this means is that you should (1) give the student a test of a set of words, (2) have each student correct his own paper, and (3) the student studies just the words missed. In fact there is usually no need to study the whole word because the mistake is just a single letter or a few letters. Then another test is given.

If there are mistakes, the student studies them and takes another test. Note that this procedure is in contrast with a procedure that we do not recommend in which the teacher first gives the students a list of words to be studied and then gives a test (the study-test procedure). There is no point in wasting time studying or drilling on words that the student already knows how to spell. Good spellers can use the time more productively to write more stories or read more books. Spelling researchers have also found that regular systematic spelling lessons create better spellers than an incidental approach (Hodges 1981).

How many words to include in a Speller which covers Grades 1 through 6 was based on tradition or, perhaps a better way to say it, based on the experience of thousands of American elementary teachers. That tradition says that 20 words a week for 35 weeks of the school year is about right. However, because lessons in grades 1 and 2 are often somewhat shorter, we have made first grade lessons only 10 words and second grade lessons only 15 words long. First grade is also a special case because the children are just experiencing formal writing lessons. Hence, there are only 20 lessons for first grade. This means that the first grade teacher can start later in the year or space the lesson out so that they occur about once every two weeks. In any event, each of the lessons is simply numbered 1 through 195. Only the chart suggests that lessons 1 through 20 are first grade. It is quite possible that some teachers or some schools will shift the lessons up or down by a grade or more.

Here is the chart which suggests how many lessons and words are to be taught at each grade level.

GRADE	WORDS PER LESSON	NUMBER OF LESSONS	TOTAL WORDS TAUGHT	LESSON NUMBERS
1	10	20	200	1 - 20
2	15	35	525	21 - 55
3	20	35	700	56 - 90
4	20	35	700	91 - 125
5	20	35	700	126 - 160
6	20	35	700	161 - 195
Totals		195	3525	

* Total words taught refers to only the main part of the lessons such as the *Instant Words* or *Picture Nouns*. Many more words are supplemental (words used in Phonogram Families and Variant Forms of the *Instant Words*, such as regular plurals and past tenses).

Hanna, Hodges, and Hanna (1971) advise:

"an effective spelling program must rest on a spirally conceived, carefully planned sequence, and that the individual teacher must bear considerable responsibility for adjusting this basic program to the various levels of maturity present in the individuals in his class." (pg 113).

I heartily agree and would furthermore like to make this advice more specific. Some schools might find it better to start formal spelling lessons in second grade, while others might start it with some pupils at the beginning of first grade or even kindergarten.

Some teachers may wish to have spelling groups like the traditional reading groups: fast, average, and slow. The slow group might take less words per lesson and therefore take more time to progress through the Spelling Book. Conversely, faster students might progress somewhat faster than the average group. However, much adjustment for a faster spelling group can be made by simply adding spelling words from other subjects, such as science or social studies, or using the Variant Forms of the *Instant Words* that are given in all lessons above Grade 2.

In addition to regular elementary grades, this spelling curriculum is also ideal for remedial, special education, disadvantaged, or ESL pupils in secondary schools, adult education classes, or tutoring situations. These pupils often need a delayed start or slower progression in a spelling program. Remember that most of the words in this spelling program are *Instant Words*, or a high frequency vocabulary. They are the most used words in writing and reading - anybody's writing or reading.

This Book Is Dedicated To

NOAH WEBSTER, LL.D.
America lexicographer
1758-1843

Noah Webster wrote the historically famous <u>Blue Backed Speller</u>, which helped millions of American Children learn to spell and to read better in one room rural schools and emerging city schools during the 1800's. The first edition of the <u>Elementary Spelling Book</u>, as it was formally called, was published in 1783, but a revision of the original was actually published up to 1908. Like Webster's famous speller, this book is essentially ungraded; the lessons are simply numbered in sequence of difficulty. This book is also similar to his book in that it contains some simple reading and writing sentences in the early lessons. But the big difference between this Spelling Book and Webster's is that the word selection and even phonics lessons are much better. Educational research has contributed a lot in recent decades. Where Webster used the simple but logical system of word grading by just increasing the number of syllables, we now have a scientific word count of millions of words done by computer so we know with a fair degree of certainty which are the "most needed" words by any child or, in fact, any writer. Linguists have also contributed to a more accurate system of phonics (phoneme-grapheme relationship). And, finally, educational research has shown that some teaching methods, such as the test-study method, is better than the study-test method.

We hope that Noah Webster, who is also the father of American dictionaries, first published in 1806, would be pleased that American educators remember his important contribution to spelling and reading education. We are certain that he would agree with today's teachers that spelling is important, in fact, a necessity for an educated person, and that regular systematic spelling lessons are far better than not teaching spelling at all or using only an unsystematic incidental approach.

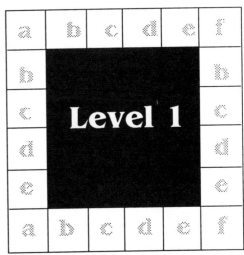

Level 1

Lessons 1-20

This Section contains 20 Lessons
Each Lesson contains:
- **10 Spelling Words**
    5 Instant Words and
    5 Picture Nouns
    Instant Words Ranks 1-100

- **Sentences or Phrases** which use these words

- **A Phonogram Family of Words**

- **Phonics** a phoneme-grapheme correspondence

- **Notes** which comment on some of the words

- **Review suggestions**

    any part of the Lesson may be omitted or
    amplified by the teacher

Instant Words 1-5   **Picture Nouns Group 1**

the

of

and

a

to

boy

girl

man

woman

baby

Phrases to read or write

a boy

the girl

man and woman

the baby of the woman

to the boy and girl

to a man and baby

Word study   Phonogram "-an"

-an

man   ran   can   pan

Note: In the word "of" it is unusual to have an "o" make the /u/ sound and the "f" make a /v/ sound. This is why "of" is a "sight" word. In fact all these words can be just "sight" words as phonics is gradually introduced.

Phonics   Short "a"

man   ran

Note: The Closed Syllable Rule states that when the syllable ends in a consonant, the single letter vowel is short.

Laguna Beach Educational Books 245 Grandview, Laguna Beach, California 92651

Instant Words 6-10   **Picture Nouns Group 2**

in

is

you

that

it

 ball

 doll

train

game

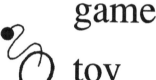

 toy

Sentences and phrases to read or write

A doll is a toy.   that ball
It is for you.   in a game
The train is a game.   It is in a doll.

Word study   Plurals "-s"

balls   games   dolls
toys   trains

Note: Sometimes a letter such as "l" in "doll" is doubled but still makes the same sound.

Phonics   Short "i"

in   is   it

Note: The closed Syllable Rule states that when the syllable ends in a consonant the single letter vowel is short.

Laguna Beach Educational Books 245 Grandview, Laguna Beach, California 92651

Instant Words 11-15   **Picture Nouns Group 3**

he	**1** one
was	two **2**
for	**3** three
on	four **4**
are	**5** five

Sentences and phrases to read or write

Two and three are five.   he is three
Four dolls are on the train.   you are four
One ball was for you.   on to the game

Word study Homophones

four	for
two	to

Note: Homophones are words that sound the same but have different spelling and different meaning.

Phonics Consonant "f"

for   four   five

Note: The /f/ sound is usually made by the letter "f", and only rarely by the letters "ph" as in "phone."

Laguna Beach Educational Books 245 Grandview, Laguna Beach, California 92651

Instant Words 16-20   **Picture Nouns Group 4**

as   shirt

with   pants

his   dress

they   shoes

I   hat

Sentences and phrases to read or write

Dress with a hat and shoes.

You can dress as a man.

It is a man with his hat.

his pants and shirt

they and I

with you

Word study Phonics Listening

Final "-s" sometimes makes /s/ sound and sometimes makes /z/ sound at the end of a word.

(final /s/)

pants

dolls

dress

(final /z/)

shoes

as

his

Note: "I" is a word because it can stand alone, has meaning and has a vowel sound. The other single letter word in English is "a" as in "a hat." Final double "ss" always makes the /s/ sound.

Phonics Consonant "s" = "z" at end of word

as   his   shoes

is   was

Review: Selected Instant Words in Lessons 1, 2 & 3.

Laguna Beach Educational Books 245 Grandview, Laguna Beach, California 92651

at	cat
be	dog
this	bird
have	fish
from	rabbit

Sentences and phrases to read or write

I have a fish and rabbit.   be at this

You can be with this bird.   have a dog

This toy is for the cat.   this is from

Word study Phonics   Phonogram "-at"
Initial consonant substitution with phonogram "-at"

-at

cat	sat	bat
hat	rat	fat

Note: All true phonograms consist of a vowel sound and a consonant sound and are less than a word. They need another consonant to be a complete word. They are one kind of "spelling pattern".

Phonics Consonant "t"

toy	to	rabbit
at	cat	

Review: Word Study in Lessons 1, 2, 3 & 4.

Laguna Beach Educational Books 245 Grandview, Laguna Beach, California 92651

or

one

had

by

words

 table

 chair

 sofa

 chest

 desk

Sentences and phrases to read or write

I had one sofa.

It is in the desk.

You have one chair.

table or chair

by the chest

with words

Word study   Phonogram "-ad"

-ad

| had | mad | bad |
| Dad | sad | pad |

Note: There are occasional duplications or words in the spelling list ("one" also appears in Lesson 3) because Picture Nouns and words in Word Study come from different sources. A little duplication and repetition doesn't hurt beginning spellers.

Phonics   Consonant "d"

desk   dog   had   words

Review: Phonics in Lessons 1-5.

Laguna Beach Educational Books 245 Grandview, Laguna Beach, California 92651

Instant Words 31-35

Picture Nouns Group 7

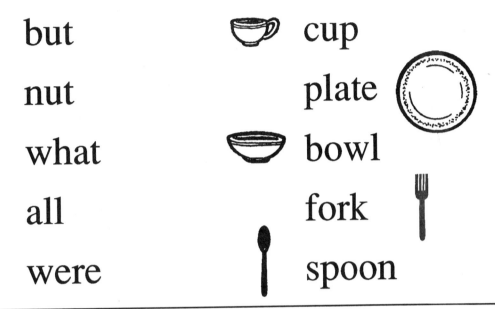

but

nut

what

all

were

cup

plate

bowl

fork

spoon

Sentences and phrases to read or write

Not the plate but the bowl.

The fork and the spoon were

all by the cup.

What is on the plate?

what cup

all the spoons

not the bowl

Word study Phonogram "-ut"

-ut

but	cut	hut
nut	gut	rut

Note: We are beginning to see silent "e" at the end of some words. When letter "e" is at the end of a word it is usually silent, hence students must remember it is there. Only sometimes does the final "e" make the preceding vowel long, (the Final "e" Rule) as in "plate", but not always as in "where", "one", or "have".

Phonics Short "u"

but

cup

nut

Review: Check Personal Spelling List.

Laguna Beach Educational Books 245 Grandview, Laguna Beach, California 92651

Instant Words 36-40 **Picture Nouns Group 8**

we  car

when truck

your  bus

can plane

said  boat

---

Sentences and phrases to read or write

The car is with the truck and bus.   we can

We can have one boat.   your plane

When is his plane in?   I said

Word study Phonogram "-en"

-en

when	hen	pen
ten	men	den

Phonics Consonant "c" = "k"

can   car   cat   cup

Note: The letter "c" has no sound of its own. Before vowels "a", "o" or "u" it frequently makes the /k/ sound. Later we will give examples that before vowels "i", "e" and "y", it frequently makes the /s/ sound - for example, "city".

Note: The /k/ sound at the end of "truck" (and a lot of other words) is spelled "ck". See Lesson 37.

Review: Selected Instant Words in Lessons 4-7.

Laguna Beach Educational Books 245 Grandview, Laguna Beach, California 92651

Instant Words 41-45   **Picture Nouns Group 9**

there   bread

use   meat

an   soup

each   apple

which   cereal

Sentences and phrases to read or write

Which cereal is yours?   meat soup
Use an apple in each.   use which bread
There are words on this one.   an apple

Word study Homophones

meat   —   meet

there   —   their

Note: "Meat" is a noun and "meet" is a verb. "There" and "their" are homophones with different meanings.

Phonics   Long "e" - Spelled "ea"

each   meat   cereal

Note: The vowel digraph (2 letters) "ea" usually makes the long /ē/ sound, but unfortunately as we see in this lesson it sometimes makes the short /ĕ/ sound as in "bread". See Lesson 32.

Review: Word Study in Lessons 5-8.

Laguna Beach Educational Books 245 Grandview, Laguna Beach, California 92651

Instant Words 46-50   **Picture Nouns Group 10**

she

do

how

their

if

 water

milk

 juice

 soda

malt

Sentences and phrases to read or write

Do you have a malt or soda?   their juice

How can she do it?   if it is milk

They had their water.   she had soda

Word study   Phonogram "-ow"

This "ow" sound is the /ou/ sound heard in "cow." The other "ow" sound /o/ heard in "know" will be taught later.

-ow

how	cow	sow
now	bow	vow

Note: "ow" is really a vowel digraph (2 letters), which is the spelling pattern of this phoneme or single speech sound.

Phonics   Consonant "m"

milk   malt   man   from

Review: Phonics in Lessons 6-9.

Laguna Beach Educational Books 245 Grandview, Laguna Beach, California 92651

Instant Words 51-55   **Picture Nouns Group 11**

will   **6** six

up   seven **7**

other   **8** eight

about   nine **9**

out   **10** ten

Sentences and phrases to read or write

She will be about six or seven.   the other eight
He will be up to eight or nine.   up to about six
Ten and you are out.   will be out

Word study   Phonogram "-ill"

-ill

will   pill   kill
bill   hill   mill

Note: "Eight" is a very un-phonetic word. The "ei" makes a long /ā/ sound and the "gh" is silent. Students need to pay careful attention to words like this.

Phonics   Consonant "s"

six   **seven**   **soda**   **soup**

Note: This is the regular sound of /s/. It always makes this /s/ sound at the beginning of a word.

Review: Check Personal Spelling Lists.

Laguna Beach Educational Books 245 Grandview, Laguna Beach, California 92651

Instant Words 56-60   **Picture Nouns Group 12**

many    fruit

then   orange

them   grape

these   pear

so   banana

Sentences and phrases to read or write

She had an orange, then   so many bananas
  these grapes.   these fruit
Have them when you can.   so then
He had so many pears.

Word study   Phonogram "-ape"

-ape

grape   shape
tape   cape

Phonics   Consonant "th" voiced

then   them   these   the

Note: The consonant digraph "th" makes two sounds. These words use the "voiced" /th/. The other /th/ sound is "voiceless", as in "thin." Voiced means your vocal cords are used in making the sound. See Lesson 29.

Review: Selected Instant Words in Lessons 8-11.

Laguna Beach Educational Books 245 Grandview, Laguna Beach, California

Instant Words 61-65   **Picture Nouns Group 13**

some    bush

her   flower

would    grass

make   plant

like   tree

Sentences and phrases to read or write

It is her plant and tree.   some flowers
I would like to make a bush.   like grass
Make some flowers.   her tree

Word study   Phonogram "-ake"

-ake

make   lake   take
cake   bake   quake

Phonics   Long "a" Final "e" Rule

make   grape   plate   game

Note: The letter "e" at the end of a word frequently makes the preceding vowel long. But not always – see the word "some" in this lesson. In any event, the final letter "e" is usually silent.

Review: Word Study in Lessons 9-12.

Laguna Beach Educational Books 245 Grandview, Laguna Beach, California 92651

Instant Words 66-70

Picture Nouns Group 14

him

 sun

into

moon

time

★ star

has

cloud

look

 rain

Sentences and phrases to read or write

It has time to rain.
Look at the moon and stars.
Look at him in the sun.

into the clouds
rain clouds
time for the moon

Word study Phonogram "-ain"

-ain

rain   pain
main   gain

Note: Even though both "moon" and "look" have double "oo", they make different sounds. "Look" has the short /ŏŏ/, which some dictionaries indicate by /u̇/ and "moon" has the long /ōo/, which some dictionaries indicate by /ü/.

Phonics Consonant "h"

him   has   her   how

Review: Phonics in Lessons 10-13.

Laguna Beach Educational Books 245 Grandview, Laguna Beach, California 92651

Instant Words 71-75   **Picture Nouns Group 15**

two   lake

more   rock

write   dirt

go   field

see   hill

Sentences and phrases to read or write

Write about the field and hill.   two lakes
See the dirt on her.   more rocks
Go to the lake.   see the field

Word study Phonogram "-ock"

-ock

rock   lock   sock   dock

Note: Watch out for the silent "w" in "write" and "two." Remember "two", "too", and "to" are homophones.

Phonics Consonant "l"

lake   hill   look
all   like   cereal

Note: Sometimes the letter "l" is doubled at the end of some words but not always. Also see Lesson 54.

Review: Check Personal Spelling Lists.

Laguna Beach Educational Books 245 Grandview, Laguna Beach, California 92651

Instant Words 76-80   **Picture Nouns Group 16**

number   horse

no   cow

way   pig

could   chicken

people   duck

Sentences and phrases to read or write

Could people see the horse?   no way
A number of cows and pigs   the chicken
  are out.   a number of ducks
People are chicken to duck.

Word study Phonogram "-ay"

-ay

way	may	jay
day	bay	hay

Note: The letters "ay" are technically a grapheme or a vowel digraph. Capital "May" is the month. Proper nouns like names use capitals for first letters.

Phonics Consonant "n"

number	sun	nine
moon	no	banana

Review: Selected Instant Words in Lessons 12-15.

Laguna Beach Educational Books 245 Grandview, Laguna Beach, California 92651

Instant Words 81-85   **Picture Nouns Group 17**

my	farmer
than	policeman
first	cook
water	doctor
been	nurse

Sentences and phrases to read or write

Go first to the nurse.   my doctor
He has been a farmer.   than a policeman
The cook had some water.   has been first

Word study Phonogram "-ook"

-ook

cook	book	hook
look	took	shook

Note: The "-er" in "farmer" is a suffix and can be taken off to make the word "farm", but you can't do that with "water" because it's not a suffix.

Phonics Consonant "p"

policeman	up	pig
soup	people	apple

Review: Word Study in Lessons 13-16.

Laguna Beach Educational Books 245 Grandview, Laguna Beach, California 92651

Instant Words 86-90   **Picture Nouns Group 18**

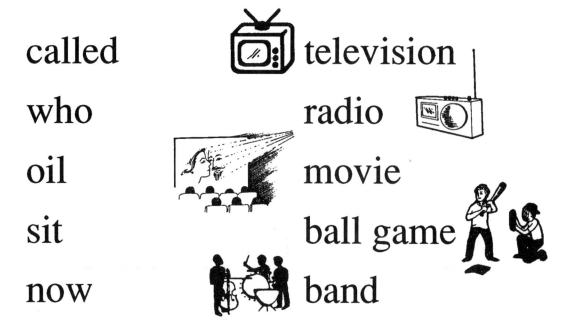

called   television

who   radio

oil   movie

sit   ball game

now   band

Sentences and phrases to read or write

Sit by the television.   who called
See the ball game and band.   oil now
Who called on the radio?   see the movie

Word study Phonogram "-all"

-all

ball	fall	tall
call	hall	wall

Note: "Ball game" is two words. We used it in the Picture Noun word group on entertainment because it covers several sports (which incidently are one word) like "football", "baseball" and "basketball".

Phonics Consonant "r"

radio	water	rock
dirt	rain	her

Review: Phonics in Lessons 14-17.

Laguna Beach Educational Books 245 Grandview, Laguna Beach, California 92651

Instant Words 91-95   **Picture Nouns Group 19**

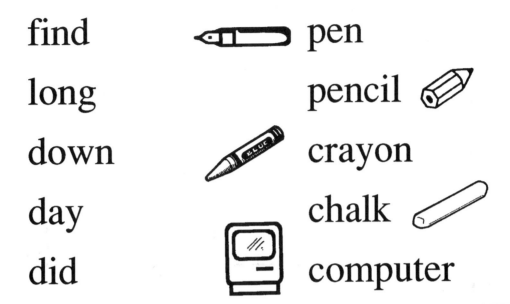

find	pen
long	pencil
down	crayon
day	chalk
did	computer

Sentences and phrases to read or write

Find your pen and pencil.　　　　long chalk
He did it all day long.　　　　　computer is down
Find the crayon and chalk.　　　computer day

Word study　Phonogram "-ind"

-ind

find　　　　mind　　　　kind　　　　wind

Note: "Wind" is a heteronym and when pronounced /wind/ means blowing air, but when it rhymes with "kind" /wind/ it means to wrap around. Heteronyms look the same but sound different.

Phonics　Long "i" Final "e" Rule

write　　　　like　　　　time
nine　　　　five

Note: The Final "e" Rule states that a silent "e" at the end of a word usually makes the preceding vowel long. But sometimes the vowel is long anyway, as in the word "find" in this lesson.

Review: Check Personal Spelling Lists

Laguna Beach Educational Books 245 Grandview, Laguna Beach, California 92651

Instant Words 96-100   **Picture Nouns Group 20**

get   book

come   newspaper

made   magazine

may   sign

part   letter

Sentences and phrases to read or write

Come and get your letter.   made a newspaper
May we get the magazine?   part of a newspaper
Sign part of the book.   a big sign

Word study   Phonogram "-et"

	-et	
get	let	set
pet	net	wet

Note: Multiple meanings: "sign" is both a verb and a noun; "letter" is both a symbol of the alphabet and a personal communication.

Phonics   Consonant "g"

get   go   game   girl

Note: This is the regular /g/ sound of the letter "g". The letter "g" has a second sound of /j/ which will be mentioned later, for example, "gem". See Lesson 55.

Review: Selected Instant Words in Lessons 16-19.

Laguna Beach Educational Books 245 Grandview, Laguna Beach, California 92651

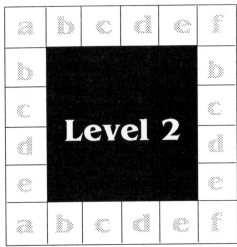

Level 2

Lessons 21-55

This Section contains 35 Lessons
Each Lesson contains:
- **15 Spelling Words**
    Instant Words Ranks 101-625

- **Sentences or Phrases** which use these words

- **A Phonogram Family of Words**

- **Phonics** a phoneme-grapheme correspondence

- **Notes** which comment on some of the words

- **Review suggestions**
    any part of the Lesson may be omitted or
    amplified by the teacher

Instant Words 101-115

over	place
new	years
sound	live
take	me
only	back
little	give
work	most
know	

Sentences to read or write

Take over the new work.
It is the only little sound I know.
Which place do you live.
Give back most of it to me.
Most years I live over there.

Word Study   Past Tense "-ed" for verbs

sounded	placed
worked	lived
backed	

Note: This is the regular rule for writing past tense. Also use this "-ed" ending when writing the past participle. The past participle uses "have, has, had", for example, "He has worked." Some verbs have an irregular past, for example, "give-gave".

Phonics

Long "o"	over	most	no
	only	go	so

Note: The Open Syllable ending rule, which states that if a vowel letter ends the syllable, the vowel is long, explains "over, go, no, so", but does not work for "only" or "most" because these are exceptions.

Laguna Beach Educational Books 245 Grandview, Laguna Beach, California 92651

Instant Words 116-130

very	**man**
after	**think**
things	**say**
our	**great**
just	**where**
name	**help**
good	**through**
sentence	

Sentences to read or write

Think of a very good name.
Our great man will help you through.
Just say good things in this sentence.
Where will you put the things after you are through?

Word Study   Suffix "-er"

greater	**helper**
thinker	**worker**

Note: The suffix "-er" on a noun means "one who does", for example, "work" + "er". The suffix "-er" on an adjective makes a comparative "comparatively more". For example, "greater" is comparatively more than "great". But for spelling of either, the regular rule is to just add "-er" to the base word. However, the final "-er" isn't always a suffix, as in "after".

Phonics

<u>Consonant "v"</u>	very	over
	have	give

Laguna Beach Educational Books 245 Grandview, Laguna Beach, California 92651

Instant Words 131-145

much	same
before	tell
line	boy
right	following
too	came
means	want
old	show
any	

Sentences to read or write

I want it very much.
The show means the same as before.
They were following us too.
He came right before any of us.

Word Study   Homophones "too", "right"   These words sound the same but have different meanings and different spellings.

too	to	two
right	write	

Homophones "two" and "to" were in Lesson 3. This Lesson adds "too".

Phonics

<u>Consonant "w"</u>	want	was	we
	woman	with	will

Note: Watch out for letter "w". It is often silent (or part of a digraph) like the "ow" in "show" or "wr" in "write".

Laguna Beach Educational Books 245 Grandview, Laguna Beach, California 92651

Instant Words 146-160

also	**does**
around	**another**
form	**well**
three	**large**
small	**must**
set	**big**
put	**even**
end	

Sentences to read or write

Put the large form around the well.
Set the small end even with this.
The big three must also be even.
Does he have another one?

Word Study   Comparative adjectives "-er" and superlative "-est"

small	smaller	smallest
large	larger	largest
big	bigger	biggest

Note: This Lesson introduces the superlative form with the "-est" ending. Note the spelling change for big: the "g" is doubled when the ending is added. For this and other endings, see Spelling Rules for explanation. At this stage, it is not advised to have students memorize Spelling Rules.

Phonics

Short "e"	end	well	chest
	set	pen	ten

Note: The syllable ending rule, which states that if the syllable ends in a consonant, the vowel is short, explains these examples well. Like all vowels, however, letter "e" has many other uses.

Review: Selected Instant Words in Lessons 21, 22 & 23.

Laguna Beach Educational Books 245 Grandview, Laguna Beach, California 92651

Instant Words 161-175

such	read
because	need
turned	land
here	different
why	home
asked	us
went	move
men	

Sentences to read or write

The men asked why we turned here.
Read to us about the move to a different land.
We went because we need a home.
Why does he have such a different home?

Word Study   Suffix "-ing"

turning	reading	asking
needing	landing	moving

Note: The "e" at the end of "move" is removed when "-ing" is added. See Spelling Rule 3 in Appendix 1 for explanation.

Phonics

Consonant "h" here	have	him
he	home	hat

Note: The letter "h" is also frequently part of a digraph like "th" or "sh", which will be taught soon. See Lessons 12, 29, 31, 46 & 52.

Review: Word Study in Lessons 21, 22, 23, & 24.

Laguna Beach Educational Books 245 Grandview, Laguna Beach, California 92651

Instant Words 176-190

try	spell
kind	air
hand	away
picture	animals
again	house
change	point
off	page
play	

Sentences to read or write

Change the picture of the house again.
Try to point to the page with one hand.
Be kind when you play with animals.
Turn the air off in the house.
Put away the picture.
Spell that word again.

Word Study   Phonogram "-and"

hand	band	land
grand	sand	stand

Note: This Lesson has "kind" and the "-ind" phonogram is in Lesson 19. This Lesson has "play" and the "-ay" digraph is in Lesson 16.

Phonics

<u>Consonant "k"</u>	kind	dark	like
	look	milk	make

Note: The /k/ sound at the beginning of many words is spelled with the letter "c" (Lesson 8), and the /k/ sound at the end of many words spelled "ck", as in "rock". See Lesson 37.

Review: Phonics in Lessons 21-25.

Laguna Beach Educational Books 245 Grandview, Laguna Beach, California 92651

Instant Words 191-205

letters	American
mother	world
answer	high
found	every
study	near
still	add
learn	food
should	

Sentences to read or write

My mother answered letters every day.
Every American should study and learn.
Add more food for the world.
We found it near the high chair.
You should still answer your mother.

Word Study   Phonogram "-ear"

near	year	clear
dear	tear	spear
hear	fear	smear

Note: This Lesson has the word "still". The "-ill" phonogram is in Lesson 11.

Phonics

Vowel digraph "ou"	found	out	about
	house	our	sound

Note: This same /ou/ sound is also spelled "ow". See Lesson 40.

Review: Check Personal Spelling Lists. Partners quiz.

Laguna Beach Educational Books 245 Grandview, Laguna Beach, California 92651

Instant Words 206-220

between	**keep**
own	**trees**
below	**never**
country	**started**
plants	**city**
last	**earth**
school	**eyes**
father	

Sentences to read or write

The earth needs trees and plants.
Father took me to my last city school.
Never keep your own eyes below it.
My own country is big.
He started to run between the trees.

Word Study   Plural for words ending in "y". Change "y" to "i" and add "es".

country	**countries**
city	**cities**

Note: See Spelling Rules in Appendix 1 for this rule (1c) and some exceptions (1d & e). Do not teach exceptions now.

Phonics

<u>**Vowel digraph "oo"**</u>	**school**	**too**
<u>**Long sound**</u>	**food**	**moon**

Note: This same long /o͞o/ sound is also spelled "u". See Lesson 50. The vowel digraph "oo" also has a short sound as in "look". See Lesson 44.

Review: Selected Instant Words in Lessons 24, 25, 26, & 27.

Laguna Beach Educational Books 245 Grandview, Laguna Beach, California 92651

Instant Words 221-235

light	few
thought	while
head	along
under	might
story	close
saw	something
left	seemed
don't	

Sentences to read or write

I thought you might want something.
The light was close to his head.
He saw the story under his book.
We have only a few left.
The word seemed right all along.
Don't run while at school.

Word Study   Phonogram "-aw"

saw	paw	law
draw	jaw	claw

Note: You may wish to get technical and call "-aw" a grapheme or digraph, which it is for the phoneme "ô". It is seen at the beginning of some words like "awful". Strictly speaking, a phonogram has a vowel and a consonant. But from a spelling standpoint, it doesn't matter what you call it, it's a Spelling Pattern.

Phonics

<u>Consonant digraph "th"</u>	thought	with	think
<u>Voiceless sound</u>	things	three	

Note: The voiced sound of "th", as in "this", was taught in Lesson 12.

Review: Word Study in Lessons 25, 26, 27, & 28.

Laguna Beach Educational Books 245 Grandview, Laguna Beach, California 92651

Instant Words 236-250

next	**both**
hard	**paper**
open	**together**
example	**got**
beginning	**group**
life	**often**
always	**run**
those	

Sentences to read or write

The next example is hard.
The paper is always open.
The group was together from the beginning.
Run for your life.
He often got both those papers.

Word Study   Phonogram "-un"

run	**gun**	**sun**
shun	**fun**	**spun**

Note: The lesson word "beginning" is taught as an Instant Word because it is more common than "begin". However, your students need to know that they can take base words out of variant forms just as they need to know that they can add on suffixes.

Phonics

<u>Consonant "b"</u>	both	beginning	about
	big	boy	baby

Review: Phonics in Lessons 26, 27, 28, & 29.

Laguna Beach Educational Books 245 Grandview, Laguna Beach, California 92651

Instant Words 251-265

important	walked
until	white
children	sea
side	began
feet	grow
car	took
miles	river
night	

Sentences to read or write

The children walked for miles at night.
The car began to go to the side of the river.
It's important that your feet began to grow.

Word Study   Phonograms "-ite", "-ight"

"-ite"		**"ight"**	
white	kite	night	fight
write	bite	right	light

Note: "Write" and "right" are homophones.

Phonics

Consonant digraph "wh"	white	why
	who	when
	what	where

Note: Digraphs like "wh" must be seen and spelled as one unit (Spelling Pattern or grapheme). It is not a blend of /w/ and /h/ sounds, but a separate speech sound (phoneme).

Review: Check Personal Spelling Lists. Partners quiz.

Laguna Beach Educational Books 245 Grandview, Laguna Beach, California 92651

Instant Words 266-280

four	second
carry	later
state	miss
once	idea
book	enough
hear	eat
stop	face
without	

Sentences to read or write

I can carry four books at once.
Stop so you can hear my second idea.
Eat later or you will miss the game.
Which state is without enough water?
Look at his face.

Word Study   Phonogram "-ate"

state	gate	date
plate	late	skate

Note: The Homophone "four - for" was in Lesson 3. The phonogram "-ook" was in Lesson 17, and "-ear" was in Lesson 27. The word "miss", if capitalized, is a title, "Miss".

Phonics

Long "e"	eat	read	near
Spelled "ea"	hear	means	sea

Note: For other spellings of the long /ē/ sound, see "e" in Lesson 41, "ee" in Lesson 39, and "y" in Lesson 33.

Review: Selected Instant Words in Lessons 28, 29, 30, & 31.

Laguna Beach Educational Books 245 Grandview, Laguna Beach, California 92651

Instant Words 281-295

watch	sometimes
far	mountains
Indians	cut
really	young
almost	talk
let	soon
above	list
girl	

Sentences to read or write

Young Indian girls always talk.
Far above the mountains it is cold.
Really watch out or you will get cut.
Write the list sometime soon.
I almost let him go.

Word Study   Phonogram "-ar"

far	bar	tar
car	jar	star

Note: The phonogram "-et" as in "let" is in Lesson 20.

Phonics

<u>Long "e"</u>	really	any	many
<u>Spelled "y"</u>	baby	very	story

Note: Letter "y" at the end of a two syllable word usually makes the long /ē/ sound. Letter "y" at the end of a one syllable word makes the long /ī/ sound, as in "my". See Lesson 45. For consonant /y/ sound, see Lesson 49.

Review: Word Study in Lessons 29, 30, 31, & 32.

Laguna Beach Educational Books 245 Grandview, Laguna Beach, California 92651

Instant Words 296-310

song	stand
being	sun
leave	questions
family	fish
it's	area
body	mark
music	dog
color	

Sentences to read or write

The dog and the fish like the song.
It's time to leave the music area.
Color the sun yellow.
Do you have any questions about your body?
For the time being stand with your family.

Word Study   Phonogram "-ark"

mark	dark	shark
park	lark	bark

Note: "Fish" is both singular and plural. It is one of the exceptions to forming plurals by adding "-s".

Phonics

Broad "o"	song	or	offer
Spelled "o"	off	for	long

Note: The different sounds of vowels are often difficult to distinguish. The broad /ô/ in "or" is different from the short /ŏ/ in "dog" or "body". See Lesson 36.

Review: Phonics in Lessons 30, 31, 32, & 33.

Laguna Beach Educational Books 245 Grandview, Laguna Beach, California 92651

Instant Words 311-325

horse	piece
birds	told
problem	usually
complete	didn't
room	friends
knew	easy
since	heard
ever	

Sentences to read or write

His friends all knew the easy problem.
The same piece of music is usually heard.
Ever since the birds told the horse, it's been bad.
He didn't have room to complete the problem.

Note: "Didn't" is a contraction for "did not".

Word Study Homophones

piece - peace
knew - new
heard - herd

Phonics

<u>Consonant "s"</u>	piece	city	once
<u>Spelled "c"</u>	since	face	place

Note: The letter "c" often makes the /s/ sound, particularly in the Spelling Pattern "ce" at the end of words or when "c" is followed by an "i", "e", or "y", as in "city". The /k/ sound of "c" as in "cat" was taught in Lesson 8.

Review: Check Personal Spelling Lists. Partners quiz.

Laguna Beach Educational Books 245 Grandview, Laguna Beach, California 92651

Instant Words 326-340

order	today
red	during
door	short
sure	better
become	best
top	however
ship	low
across	

Sentences to read or write

Today you can become the best.
The red ship is better than the old one.
Use the low door for short boys.
However, you should keep order during the day.
Be sure the top part is across the number.

Note: "However" is a compound word of "how" + "ever".

Word Study   Phonogram "-ip"

ship	lip	dip
chip	tip	drip

Phonics

<u>Short "o"</u>	top	got	body
	stop	dog	

Note: Remember the Syllable Ending Rule, which states that if the syllable ends in a consonant, the vowel is often short.

Review: Selected Instant Words in Lessons 32, 33, 34, & 35.

Laguna Beach Educational Books 245 Grandview, Laguna Beach, California 92651

Instant Words 341-355

hours	waves
black	reached
products	listen
happened	wind
whole	rock
measure	space
remember	covered
early	

Sentences to read or write

The whole black rock is covered.
Remember to listen to the wind and waves.
What happened in the early hours?
Measure the space between the products.
He reached for the covered space.

Word Study   Phonogram "-ack"

black	sack	smack
jack	quack	tack

Note: The phonogram "-ock" in "rock" was in Lesson 15. The word "wind" is a heteronym, which has two pronunciations and two meanings.   "The wind is blowing", and "wind the clock".

Phonics

Consonant "k"	black	truck	back
Spelled "ck"	rock	duck	chicken

Note: At the end of a word or syllable, the /k/ sound is frequently spelled "ck" as in "black". But not always, as in "work". For /k/ sound, spelled "k", see Lesson 26, and spelled "c", see Lesson 8.

Review: Word Study in Lessons 33, 34, 35, & 36.

Laguna Beach Educational Books 245 Grandview, Laguna Beach, California 92651

Instant Words 356-370

fast	**passed**
several	**vowel**
hold	**true**
himself	**hundred**
toward	**against**
five	**pattern**
step	**numeral**
morning	

Sentences to read or write

Five hundred men passed the house.
Several vowels are in that pattern.
Hold fast against the big wind.
Step toward the morning.
He gave the numeral "one" to himself.
Can it be true?

Note: "Himself" is a compound word of "him" + "self".

Word Study Phonogram "-old"

hold	**fold**	**cold**
bold	**told**	**gold**

Phonics

Consonant "ng"	**morning**	**young**	**sing**
	song	**long**	**things**

Note: The consonant digraph makes the /ng/ sound heard at the end of a word like "sing". It is usually at the end of a word. The /ng/ sound is not a "blend". (Note how your mouth is different when making an /n/ and a /g/.)

Review: Phonics in Lessons 34, 35, 36, & 37.

Laguna Beach Educational Books 245 Grandview, Laguna Beach, California 92651

Instant Words 371-385

table	voice
north	seen
slowly	cold
money	cried
map	plan
farm	notice
pulled	south
draw	

Sentences to read or write

Plan to go slowly north and south.
Draw a map on the farm table.
She cried when the cold money was seen.
Notice that her voice cried out.
The train slowly pulled out.

Word Study   Phonogram "-ap"

map	sap	slap
cap	tap	trap

Note: The phonogram (grapheme) "-aw" in "draw" was in Lesson 29. The phonogram "-old" in "cold" was in Lesson 38. The phonogram "-an" in "plan" was in Lesson 1.

Phonics

<u>Long "e"</u>	seen	need	tree
<u>Spelled "ee"</u>	there	see	keep

Note: The long /ē/ sound spelled "ea" as in "eat" is in Lesson 9, and spelled "y" as in "carry" is in Lesson 33.

Review: Check Personal Spelling Lists. Partners quiz.

Laguna Beach Educational Books 245 Grandview, Laguna Beach, California 92651

Instant Words 386-400

sing	figure
war	certain
ground	field
fall	travel
king	wood
town	fire
I'll	upon
unit	

Sentences to read or write

A certain king had a ground war.
I'll sing in town and in the field.
He put the wood upon the fire.
The unit traveled in the fall.
Can you figure it out?

Note: "-ing" was a suffix in Lesson 25. Here it is a phonogram in "king" and "sing".

Word Study   Phonogram "-own"

town	brown	gown
down	frown	clown

Phonics

Vowel diphthong "ou"	town	now	however
Spelled "ow"	how	vowel	

Note: The diphthong sound /ou/ is sometimes spelled "ow", as in "town". But the /ou/ sound is also spelled "ou", as in "out". See Lesson 27.

Review: Selected Instant Words in Lessons 36, 37, 38, & 39.

Laguna Beach Educational Books 245 Grandview, Laguna Beach, California 92651

Instant Words 401-415

done	finally
English	wait
road	correct
half	oh
ten	quickly
fly	person
gave	became
box	

Sentences to read or write

Oh, that person is half English.
He finally gave me the correct box.
After the wait, the road was quickly opened.
All ten roads are finally done.
The fly became a person.

Note: If the word ends in "e", it is always silent, for example, "done", and sometimes it makes the preceding vowel long, such as "gave".

Word Study   Adverb suffix "-ly"   To make an adjective (word that modifies a noun) into an adverb (word that modifies a verb), usually just add "-ly".

final   + ly = finally
quick   + ly = quickly
correct + ly = correctly

Phonics

Long "e"	became	below	he
Spelled "e"	me	she	we

Note: The Open Syllable Rule states that if the syllable ends with a single vowel, it usually has the long sound. Other long /ē/ in Lessons 39, 9-33.

Review: Word Study in Lessons 37, 38, 39, & 40.

Laguna Beach Educational Books 245 Grandview, Laguna Beach, California 92651

Instant Words 416-430

shown	inches
minutes	street
strong	decided
verb	contain
stars	course
front	surface
feel	produce
fact	

Sentences to read or write

Of course I decided to feel strong.
Can you produce stars on the surface?
The fact is the street can contain more cars.
The verb was shown for three minutes.
The front is strong.

Word Study   Phonogram "-eel"

feel	heel	wheel
peel	steel	reel

Note: These phonogram words contain an unusually large number of homophones:

heel-part of foot	peel-skin
heal-cure	peal-ringing
steel-metal	reel-spool
steal-take illegally	real-true

Phonics

<u>Broad "a"</u>	stars	farmer	started
<u>Spelled "a(r)"</u>	farm	car	far

Note: The letter "a" followed by the letter "r" usually makes the broad /ä/ sound, as in "far".

Review: Phonics in Lessons 38, 39, 40, & 41.

Laguna Beach Educational Books 245 Grandview, Laguna Beach, California 92651

Instant Words 431-445

building	**inside**
ocean	**wheels**
class	**stay**
note	**green**
nothing	**known**
rest	**island**
carefully	**week**
scientists	

Sentences to read or write

Stay for a week inside this building.
Rest carefully on a green ocean island.
The note means nothing to scientists.
You have known this class a long time.

Note: The "k" before "n" in the spelling word "known" is silent. We also saw this in earlier words "know" and "knew".

Word Study   Phonogram "-ass"

class	**glass**	**brass**
pass	**grass**	**bass**

Phonics

<u>Long "o"</u>	**known**	**grow**	**own**
<u>Spelled "ow"</u>	**low**	**below**	**following**

Note: The vowel digraph "ow" sometimes makes the long /ō/ sound, as in "own". Unfortunately "ow" also sometimes makes the /ou/ sound as in "how", see Lesson 40. Long /ō/ sound spelled "o" is in Lesson 21.

Review: Check Personal Spelling Lists. Partners quiz.

Laguna Beach Educational Books 245 Grandview, Laguna Beach, California 92651

Instant Words 446-460

less	**ran**
machine	**round**
base	**boat**
ago	**game**
stood	**force**
plane	**brought**
system	**understand**
behind	

Sentences to read or write

Two is less than three.
He stood behind the base.
Try to understand the force in the system.
She brought the machine to the boat.
The plane ran fast long ago.
The game has a round ball.

Word Study   Phonogram "-ane"

plane	**cane**	**lane**
crane	**Jane**	**sane**

Note: "Jane" is capitalized because it is a proper noun. (A proper noun is the name of a person, place or thing.)

Phonics

Short "oo"	stood	good	took
	look	wood	book

Note: The vowel digraph "oo" sometimes makes the short /ŏŏ/ sound, as in "look". Unfortunately "oo" sometimes makes the long /o͞o/ sound, as in "moon", see Lesson 28.

Review: Selected Instant Words in Lessons 40, 41, 42, & 43.

Laguna Beach Educational Books 245 Grandview, Laguna Beach, California 92651

Instant Words 461-475

warm	**deep**
common	**thousands**
bring	**yes**
explain	**clear**
dry	**equation**
though	**yet**
language	**government**
shape	

Sentences to read or write

Don't go yet, wait for it to dry.
Why is it warm thousands of feet deep?
The government needs to use clear language.
Though the equation is common, it is hard to explain.
Yes, bring me the round shape.

Word Study   Phonogram "-eep"

deep	**weep**	**steep**
keep	**sheep**	**sweep**

Note: The silent letters in "though". Often the "gh" is silent, as we have seen in "right", "brought".

Phonics

Long "i"	**dry**	**my**	**try**
Spelled "y"	**try**	**by**	**fly**

Note: The single letter "y" at the end of a one syllable word frequently makes the long /ī/ sound as in "dry". The single letter "y" at the end of a polysyllabic word makes the long /ē/ sound as in "funny". See Lesson 33. In the middle of a word, "y" makes the long /ī/ sound as in "cycle".

Review: Word Study in Lessons 41, 42, 43, & 44.

Laguna Beach Educational Books 245 Grandview, Laguna Beach, California 92651

Instant Words 476-490

filled	**among**
heat	**noun**
full	**power**
hot	**cannot**
check	**able**
object	**six**
am	**size**
rule	

Sentences to read or write

Full power makes the object hot.
Check the rule about nouns.
I am a size six.
Heat the cup or it cannot be filled.
Who among you is the most able?

Word Study   Phonogram "-eat"

heat	**neat**	**wheat**
beat	**seat**	**cheat**

Note: "Object" is a heteronym, the same spelling with different pronunciation and different meanings, as in "don't object" and "the object".

Phonics

<u>**Consonant digraph "ch"**</u>	**check**	**much**	**change**
	chair	**which**	**chest**

Note: For the other consonant digraphs, see Lesson 31-"wh", Lesson 52-"sh", and Lessons 12 & 29-"th".

Review: Phonics in Lessons 42, 43, 44, & 45.

Laguna Beach Educational Books 245 Grandview, Laguna Beach, California 92651

Instant Words 491-505

dark	**include**
ball	**built**
material	**can't**
special	**matter**
heavy	**square**
fine	**syllables**
pair	**perhaps**
circle	

Sentences to read or write

He built a fine house.
Include the dark ball in the square.
It can't matter that the special material is heavy.
Perhaps you should circle the pair of syllables.

Note: "Can't" is a contraction of "can not".

Word Study   Phonogram "-ine"

fine	**line**	**mine**
dine	**nine**	**shine**

Phonics

<u>Long "a"</u>	**pair**	**air**	**contain**
<u>Spelled "ai"</u>	**wait**	**chair**	**rain**

Note: For other long /ā/ sounds, see "a-e"-Lesson 13 and "ay"-Lesson 16.

Review: Check Personal Spelling Lists. Partners quiz.

Laguna Beach Educational Books 245 Grandview, Laguna Beach, California 92651

Instant Words 506-520

bill	**anything**
felt	**divided**
suddenly	**general**
test	**energy**
direction	**subject**
center	**Europe**
farmers	**moon**
ready	

Sentences to read or write

The test was about the general subject of Europe.
The center of the moon is in that direction.
He suddenly felt ready for anything.
The two farmers divided the bill.

Note: "Anything" is a compound word of "any" + "thing".

Word Study   Proper nouns and titles are capitalized

Bill	**Mr. Farmer**	**Europe**	**General Moon**

Phonics

<u>Schwa (ə)</u>	farmer	vowel	divided
<u>Spelled "e"</u>	power	listen	turned

Note: The schwa sound /ə/ can be made by any vowel letter in an unaccented syllable. These examples show the schwa sound /ə/ made by the letter "e". The unaccented syllable is frequently at the end of a word, but it can be any place. See Lesson 54.

Review: Selected Instant Words in Lessons 44, 45, 46, & 47.

Laguna Beach Educational Books 245 Grandview, Laguna Beach, California 92651

Instant Words 521-535

region	**paint**
return	**mind**
believe	**love**
dance	**cause**
members	**rain**
picked	**exercise**
simple	**eggs**
cells	

Sentences to read or write

I believe the rain dance caused rain.
Return the eggs if you don't mind.
The members picked the paint color.
I love simple exercise.
That region is divided into many cells.

Note: The "rain" phonogram "-ain" was in Lesson 14, the "mind" phonogram "-ind" was in Lesson 19.

Word Study   Phonogram "-ell"

cell	**fell**	**tell**
bell	**sell**	**well**

Phonics

<u>Consonant "y"</u>   yes   you   young
                yet   your

Note: The consonant /y/ sound is usually spelled "y" and appears at the beginning of a word. In the middle of a word ("cycle") or at the end of a one syllable word, the letter "y" makes the long /ī/ sound as in "my", see Lesson 45. At the end of a polysyllabic word, the letter "y" makes the long /ē/ sound as in "funny". See Lesson 33.

Review: Word Study in Lessons 45, 46, 47, & 48.

Laguna Beach Educational Books 245 Grandview, Laguna Beach, California 92651

Instant Words 536-550

train	heart
blue	sit
wish	sum
drop	summer
developed	wall
window	forest
difference	probably
distance	

Sentences to read or write

Sit by the blue window.
There is probably a difference in distance.
I wish to sit on a train this summer.
The heart of the forest is well developed.
Drop it over the wall.
The sum of 2 and 2 is 4.

Note: Sometimes the final /t/ sound is made by "ed", as in "developed", and sometimes it is made by "t" as in "heart" or "forest".

Word Study   Phonogram "-um"

sum	gum	drum
bum	hum	plum

Phonics

Long "oo"	blue	numeral	through
Spelled "u"	true	rule	produce

Note: This phonics correspondence, letter "u" making the /o͞o/ sound is sometimes more phonics than even adult good spellers know, so don't worry if children have trouble with it. The /o͞o/ sound is usually made by the letters "oo", as in "moon", Lesson 28. It is not quite the same as the long /ū/ sound in "use".

Review: Phonics in Lessons 46, 47, 48, & 49.

Laguna Beach Educational Books 245 Grandview, Laguna Beach, California 92651

Instant Words 551-565

legs	kept
sat	interest
main	arms
winter	brother
wide	race
written	present
length	beautiful
reason	

Sentences to read or write

She sat on the wide chair.
His main interest last winter was to race.
She kept her brother's present.
The length of his legs and arms was too long.
The written reason was beautiful.

Note: Watch out for the silent "w" before "r" in "write" and "written".

Word Study   Phonogram "-ide"

wide	hide	slide
ride	side	bride

Phonics

Short "u" or "ə" Spelled "o"	Short "u"		Schwa "ə"	
	brother	done	second	contain
	love	money	person	direction

Note: It is very difficult to distinguish between the short /ŭ/ sound and the schwa /ə/ sound. The only real difference is whether the vowel letter making the sound is in an accented syllable or an unaccented syllable. This is for teacher information and dictionary understanding, not for children to memorize. This Lesson shows how the letter "o" makes both the short /ŭ/ and the schwa /ə/.

Review: Check Personal Spelling Lists. Partners quiz.

Laguna Beach Educational Books 245 Grandview, Laguna Beach, California 92651

Instant Words 566-580

store	**wild**
job	**happy**
edge	**beside**
past	**gone**
sign	**sky**
record	**glass**
finished	**million**
discovered	

Sentences to read or write

Put the glass just past the edge.
The sign for the job in the store was gone.
He discovered she was wild and happy.
They finished a million glasses.
She kept a record of the sky colors.

Note: "Record" is a heteronym (two pronunciations and two meanings) as in "phonograph record" (noun), and "record this music" (verb).

Word Study   **Phonogram "-ast"**

past	**mast**	**fast**
last	**blast**	**cast**

Phonics

<u>**Consonant digraph "sh"**</u>	**show**	**short**
	shoe	**should**

Note: This is the last of the consonant digraphs. The other consonant digraphs are "ch"-Lesson 46, "wh"-Lesson 31, and "th"(voiced)-Lesson 12, and "th"(voiceless)-Lesson 29.

Review: Selected Instant Words in Lessons 48, 49, 50, & 51.

Instant Words 581-595

west	paragraph
lay	raised
weather	represent
root	soft
instruments	whether
meet	clothes
third	flowers
months	

Sentences to read or write

The flowers were raised in the third month.
The roots of the weather lay in the west.
Whether to have soft clothes or instruments is her problem.
In the story they meet in the third paragraph.
Flowers represent love.

Note: It is optional if "whether" is pronounced exactly the same as "weather" (/w/ at the beginning), or if it is pronounced with a /hw/ sound at the beginning.

Word Study   Homophones

meat   =   meet   flower   =   flour

Phonics

Consonant "z"   zoo   size
                          zone   zero

Note: The /z/ sound is more often made by the letter "s" as in "has". See Lesson 4.

Review: Word Study in Lessons 49, 50, 51, & 52.

Laguna Beach Educational Books 245 Grandview, Laguna Beach, California 92651

Instant Words 596-610

shall	appear
teacher	metal
held	son
describe	either
drive	ice
cross	sleep
speak	village
solve	

Sentences to read or write

Shall the teacher appear in the village?
The son will describe either the metal or the ice.
Don't speak when you cross the drive.
The metal held together.
Solve it while you sleep.

Note: "Sun" is a homophone of "son".

Word Study   Phonogram "-eak"

speak	peak	creak
leak	weak	streak

Phonics

<u>Final "l" (əl)</u>	**"al"**		**"le"**	
<u>Spelled "al" or "le"</u>	metal	general	simple	whole
	several	cereal	table	example

Note: The final "l" is really the syllabic "l" or schwa /ə/, plus /l/ sound at the end of a polysyllabic word. The final syllable is unaccented. In single syllable words, the final /l/ sound is usually spelled "ll", as in "shall", "ball", or "doll".

Review: Phonics in Lessons 50, 51, 52, & 53.

Laguna Beach Educational Books 245 Grandview, Laguna Beach, California 92651

Instant Words 611-625

factors	**pushed**
result	**baby**
jumped	**buy**
snow	**century**
ride	**outside**
care	**everything**
floor	**tall**
hill	

Sentences to read or write

The snow is on the tall hill.
The baby jumped on the flower.
Take care if you ride outside.
Buy everything this century.
The result was he pushed all factors.

Note: There are two compound words in this Lesson: "outside" and "everything".

Word Study   Phonogram "-are"

care	**rare**	**square**
bare	**share**	**dare**

Phonics

<u>**Consonant "j"**</u>   **jumped**   **just**
                            enjoy   **subject**

Note: The /j/ sound is also made by the letter "g" when it is followed by an "i", "e", or "y", as in "giant", "gem", or "gym".

Review: Check Personal Spelling Lists. Partners quiz.

Laguna Beach Educational Books 245 Grandview, Laguna Beach, California 92651

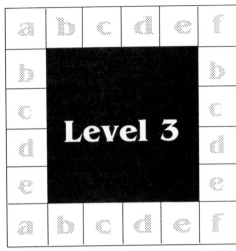

Level 3

Lessons 56-90

This Section contains 35 Lessons
Each Lesson contains:
- **20 Spelling Words**
  Instant Words Ranks 626-1325

- **Variant forms** of these words

- **Word Study**

- **Notes**

- **Review suggestions**
  you may wish to review the phonics parts
  of Lessons 1-55 during this section;
  any part of the Lesson may be omitted or
  amplified by the teacher

Instant Words 626-645

already	laughed
instead	nation
phrase	quite
soil	type
bed	themselves
copy	temperature
free	bright
hope	lead
spring	everyone
case	method

Word Study   Compound words

everyone	sometimes
themselves	something

Note: Compound words put 2 words together to form a new word.

Variant forms

phrased   phrases   phrasing
bedded   bedding   beds
freed   freeing   freely   freer   frees
springing   springs
laugh   laughing   laughs
typed   types   typing
brighter   brightest   brightly
methods

soiled   soils
copied   copies   copying
hoped   hopes   hoping
cases   casing
nations
temperatures
leading   leads

Review: Start students keeping a Personal Spelling List, see Appendix 5 for suggestions.

Laguna Beach Educational Books 245 Grandview, Laguna Beach, California 92651

Instant Words 646-665

section	although
lake	per
consonant	broken
within	moment
dictionary	tiny
hair	possible
age	gold
amount	milk
scale	quiet
pounds	natural

Word Study   Phonics "kw" sound spelled "qu"

quiet	square
quickly	question

Note: The letter "q" always appears with a "u" and "qu" makes the /kw/ sound.

Variant forms

sectioned sectioning sections	lakes
consonants	hairs
aged ages aging	amounted amounting
scaled scales scaling	amounts
broke	pound pounded
broke	pounding
tinier tiniest	moments
naturally naturalness	milked milker milking
quieted quieter quietest quietly	milks
quietness quiets	

Review: Most of the major phonics rules (correspondences between sound and spelling) are covered in Lessons 1-55. A review of them is good for anybody - student or teacher.

Laguna Beach Educational Books 245 Grandview, Laguna Beach, California 92651

Instant Words 666-685

lot	rolled
stone	bear
act	wonder
build	smiled
middle	angle
speed	fraction
count	Africa
cat	killed
someone	melody
sail	bottom

Word Study   Phonics Long "o" sound spelled "o-e"

stone	those
note	close

Note: These examples follow the Final "e" Rule - "e" at the end of a word makes the preceding vowel long - sometimes.

Variant forms

lots
acted acting acts
counted counting counts
roll rolling rolls
smile smiles smiling
fractions
African Africans
bottoming bottoms

stoned stones
speeded speeding speeds
sailed sailing sails
wondered wondering
wonderingly wonders
angles
melodies
kill killing kills

Review: The Word Study section of Lessons 1-55 contain many common phonograms. More phonograms and some phonics and spelling patterns are given in the future Word Study sections.

Laguna Beach Educational Books 245 Grandview, Laguna Beach, California 92651

Instant Words 686-705

trip	remain
hole	dress
poor	iron
let's	couldn't
fight	fingers
surprise	row
French	least
died	catch
beat	climbed
exactly	wrote

Word Study   Contractions

let's = let us   didn't = did not
couldn't = could not   she'll = she will

Note: In contractions the apostrophe shows where the missing letters could have been.

Variant forms

tripped tripping trips   holes
poorer poorest   fighting fights
surprised surprises surprising   die dies
beating beatings beats   exact exacted exactness
remained remaining remains   dressed dresses ironed
ironed ironing irons   dressing dressings
finger fingered fingering   rowed rowing rows
catches catching   climb climbing climbs

Review: Selected Instant Words in Lessons 56-58. It will be suggested that you review the Instant Words for the preceding 3 Lessons every 3rd Lesson.

Laguna Beach Educational Books 245 Grandview, Laguna Beach, California 92651

Instant Words 706-725

shouted	foot
continued	law
itself	ears
else	grass
plains	you're
gas	grew
England	skin
burning	valley
design	cents
joined	key

Word Study   Phonics /o͞o/ sound spelled "-ew"

grew	few	chew
new	knew	flew

Note: In these words the /o͞o/ sound is spelled "ew". Other ways of spelling the /o͞o/ sound are
          "oo" (Lesson 28) as in "moon" or "u" as in "truth" (Lesson 50).

Variant forms

shout shouting shouts
plain plainer plainest
plainly plainness
Englanders
designed designing designs
footless
ear
skins
cent

continue continues
continuing
gases
burn burned burns
join joining joins
laws
grasses
valleys
keyed keying keys

Review: Word Study in Lesson 56, 57, 58, & 59.

Laguna Beach Educational Books 245 Grandview, Laguna Beach, California 92651

Instant Words 726-745

president	save
brown	experiment
trouble	engine
cool	alone
cloud	drawing
lost	east
sent	pay
symbols	single
wear	touch
bad	information

Word Study   Phonogram "-one"

alone	cone	stone
lone	bone	phone

Note: This phonogram conforms to the Final "e" Rule in Lesson 58.

Variant forms

presidents
troubled troubles troubling
cooled cooler coolest
coolly coolness cools
wearer wearers wearing wears
saved saver saves saving savings
engines
drawings
paying pays
touched touches touching

browned browner
brownest browning
clouded clouds
symbol
badly badness
experimented experimenter
experimenters
experimenting
experiments
singled singles

Review: Check to make sure each student is keeping a Personal Spelling List. Partners can quiz each other from their Personal Spelling Lists.

Laguna Beach Educational Books 245 Grandview, Laguna Beach, California 92651

Instant Words 746-765

express	rise
mouth	statement
yard	stick
equal	party
decimal	seeds
yourself	suppose
control	woman
practice	coast
report	bank
straight	period

Word Study   Phonogram "-ess"

express	less	bless
dress	mess	guess

Note: The final /s/ sound is sometimes spelled "ss" but more often it is just spelled with one "s" as in "hats" (Lesson 11).

Variant forms

expressed expresses expressing   mouths
yards   decimals
parties   equaled equaling
controllable controlled   equally equals
controlling controls   practiced practices
reported reportedly   practicing
reporting reports   straighter
risen rises rising   statements
sticking sticks   seed seeding
supposes supposing   coasted coasting coasts
banked banking banks   periods

Review: Instant Words in Lessons 59, 60, & 61.

Laguna Beach Educational Books 245 Grandview, Laguna Beach, California 92651

Instant Words 766-785

wire	caught
choose	fell
clean	team
visit	God
bit	captain
whose	direct
received	ring
garden	serve
please	child
strange	desert

Word Study   Phonogram "-ean"

clean	bean	lean
mean	Jean	Dean

Note: This phonogram conforms to the phonics correspondence where the sound of long /ē/ is spelled "ea" in Lesson 9.

Variant forms

wired   wires   wiring
cleaned   cleaner   cleaners
cleaning   cleans
gods
receive   receives   receiving
pleased   pleases   pleasing
teamed   teams
directed   directing   directly
directness   directs
served   serves
serving   servings

choosing
visited   visiting   visits
bits
captains
gardening   gardens
strangely   strangeness
strangest
ringed   ringer   ringers
ringing   rings
deserted   deserters
deserting   desertion   deserts

Review: Word Study in Lessons 60, 61, & 62.

Laguna Beach Educational Books 245 Grandview, Laguna Beach, California **92651**

Instant Words 786-805

increase	lady
history	students
cost	human
maybe	art
business	feeling
separate	supply
break	corner
uncle	electric
hunting	insects
flow	crops

Word Study   Spelling Pattern "-or"

history	for	horn
corner	more	sore

Note: When the letter "o" is followed by "r" it usually has the broad /ô/ sound. For other broad /ô/'s, see Lesson 34.

Variant forms

increased increases increasing
increasingly
businesses
breaking breaks
uncles
insect
flowed flowing flows
student
arts
cornered cornering corners
electrical electrically electrics

histories
costing costs
separated separately
separates separating
feelings
hunt hunted hunts
ladies
humans
supplied suppliers
supplies supplying
crop cropped cropping

Review: Check Personal Spelling List. Partners quiz.

Laguna Beach Educational Books 245 Grandview, Laguna Beach, California 92651

Instant Words 806-825

tone	board
hit	modern
sand	compound
doctor	mine
provide	wasn't
thus	fit
won't	addition
cook	belong
bones	safe
tail	soldiers

Word Study   Spelling Pattern "-tion"

addition	direction	information
question	fraction	nation

Note: The sound /sh/ is frequently spelled "ti" in the Spelling Pattern "tion" that is at the end of many words. It is often a suffix (or morpheme) that makes a verb into a noun.

Variant forms

tones	bone
additions	soldier
sanded sanding sands	doctoring doctors
provided provides providing	cooked cooking cooks
tailless tails	boarded boarding boards
compounded compounding compounds	mined mines mining
fits fitted	belonged belonging
safely safer safest	belongs

Review: Selected Instant Words in Lessons 62, 63, & 64.

Laguna Beach Educational Books 245 Grandview, Laguna Beach, California 92651

Instant Words 826-845

guess	except
silent	expect
trade	flat
rather	seven
compare	interesting
crowd	sense
poem	string
enjoy	blow
elements	famous
indicate	value

Word Study   Phonics "x"; sound /eks/ spelled "ex"

except	explain	example
expect	express	exactly

Note: There is no specific "x" sound (phoneme), but the letter "x" is often used in the "ex" Spelling
         Pattern to make the /eks/ sound. At the end of a word "x" makes the /ks/ sound as in "box".

Variant forms

guessed guesser guesses guessing
poems
sevens
compared   compares   comparing
enjoyed   enjoying   enjoys
excepted   excepting
expected   expecting   expects
interestingly
stringed   stringing   strings
valued   values

silently
element
traded   trades   trading
crowded crowding crowds
indicated   indicates
indicating
flatly flatness flats
senses sensing
blowing   blows

Review: Word Study in Lessons 63, 64, & 65.

Laguna Beach Educational Books 245 Grandview, Laguna Beach, California 92651

Instant Words 846-865

wings	**fun**
movement	**loud**
pole	**consider**
exciting	**suggested**
branches	**thin**
thick	**position**
blood	**entered**
lie	**fruit**
spot	**tied**
bell	**rich**

Word Study   Phonogram "-ing"

wing	**bring**	**king**
sing	**thing**	**spring**

Note: For "ing" as a suffix or morpheme see Lesson 25.

Variant forms

wing winged winging wingless	poled poles poling
excite excited excitedly excites	branch branched
thicker thickest thickly	branching
thickness thicknesses	bloods
bells	fruits
movements	lied lies
spots spotted spotting	louder loudest
considered considers	loudly loudness
suggest suggesting suggests	thinly thinned thinner
positional positioned positions	thinness thinning thins
enter entering enters	tie ties
richer richest richly richness	

Review: Check Personal Spelling Lists. Partners quiz.

Laguna Beach Educational Books 245 Grandview, Laguna Beach, California 92651

Instant Words 866-885

dollars	major
send	observe
sight	tube
chief	necessary
Japanese	weight
stream	meat
planets	lifted
rhythm	process
eight	army
science	hat

Word Study   Phonogram "-end"

send	lend	blend
bend	spend	mend

Note: This phonogram conforms to the Closed Syllable Rule, which states that if the syllable ends in a consonant the vowel is usually short. Also notice all the silent "gh"'s in three of these words: "sight, eight, & weight".

Variant forms

dollar
planet
eights
sighted sighting
sightings sights
streamed streaming streams
tubes
armies
observed observer observers
observes observing
processed processes processing

Japan
rhythms
sender senders
sending sends
chiefly chiefs
sciences
meats
majoring majors
weighted weights
lift lifting lifts
hats hatter

Review: Selected Instant Words in Lessons 65, 66, & 67.

Laguna Beach Educational Books 245 Grandview, Laguna Beach, California 92651

Instant Words 886-905

property	block
particular	spread
swim	cattle
terms	wife
current	sharp
park	company
sell	radio
shoulder	we'll
industry	action
wash	capital

Word Study   Phonogram "-ead"

spread	head	lead
dead	read	bread

Note: Both "read" & "lead" are heteronyms. Each has a different pronunciation: /lĕd/-/lēd/ & /rĕd/-/rēd/ and different meaning.

Variant forms

properties
swimmer swimmers swimming swims
currents
selling sells
industries
companies
capitals
blocked blocker blocking blocks
sharper sharpest sharply sharpness
radioed radios

particularly particulars
term termed
parked parking parks
shouldered shouldering
shoulders
actions
washed washes washing
spreader spreading
spreads

Review: Word Study in Lessons 66, 67, & 68.

Laguna Beach Educational Books 245 Grandview, Laguna Beach, California 92651

Instant Words 906-925

factories	chance
settled	born
yellow	level
isn't	triangle
southern	molecules
truck	France
fair	repeated
printed	column
wouldn't	western
ahead	church

Word Study   Phonogram "-ance"

chance	dance	lance
France	glance	prance

Note: There are 2 contractions in this list: "isn't" and "wouldn't".

Variant forms

factory

yellowing yellows

fairer fairest fairly fairness

chanced chances

triangles

repeat repeatedly repeating repeats

westerns

settle settles settling

trucked trucking trucks

print printing prints

leveled leveling levels

molecule

columns

churches

Review: Check Personal Spelling Lists. Partners quiz.

Laguna Beach Educational Books 245 Grandview, Laguna Beach, California 92651

Instant Words 926-945

sister	solution
oxygen	fresh
plural	shop
various	suffix
agreed	especially
opposite	shoes
wrong	actually
chart	nose
prepared	afraid
pretty	dead

Word Study   Phonics "x" (/ks/ sound spelled "x")

oxygen	six	box
suffix	mix	fox

Note: The use of "x" in the "ex" Spelling Pattern was in Lesson 66.

Variant forms

sisters
variously
oppositely   opposites
charted   charting   charts
prettier   prettiest   prettily
solutions
shoe
fresher   freshest   freshly   freshness
suffixes
noses   nosing   shops

plurals
agree   agreeing   agrees
wronged   wrongly   wrongs
prepare   prepares
preparing
especial
actual
shopped   shopper
shoppers   shopping   nosed

Review: Selected Instant Words in Lessons 68, 69, & 70.

Laguna Beach Educational Books 245 Grandview, Laguna Beach, California 92651

Instant Words 946-965

sugar	**stretched**
adjective	**experience**
fig	**rose**
office	**allow**
huge	**fear**
gun	**workers**
similar	**Washington**
death	**Greek**
score	**women**
forward	**bought**

Word Study   Phonogram "-ore"

score	**shore**	**sore**
more	**store**	**core**

Note: The Spelling Pattern "or" was in Lesson 64.

Variant forms

sugared sugars   adjectives
figs   offices
hugely   gunned guns
similarly   deaths
scored scorer scores scoring   forwards
stretch stretches stretching   experienced experiences
roses   experiencing
allowed allowing allows   feared fearing fears
worker   Greeks

Review: Word Study in Lessons 69, 70, & 71.

Laguna Beach Educational Books 245 Grandview, Laguna Beach, California 92651

Instant Words 966-985

led	total
march	deal
northern	determine
create	evening
British	nor
difficult	rope
match	cotton
win	apple
doesn't	details
steel	entire

Word Study   Capitalization

British	Greek	Mr. Smith
France	Washington	Dr. Fry

Note: Proper nouns (specific person, places or things) start with a capital letter.

Variant forms

marched   marchers   marches
matched   matches   matching
steels
totaled   totaling   totally   totals
determined   determinedly
determines   determining
cottons   cottony
apples
entirely

created   creates   creating
winner   winners
winning   wins
dealer   dealers   deals
evenings
roped   roper   ropers
ropes   roping
detail   detailed

Review: Check Personal Spelling Lists. Partners quiz.

Laguna Beach Educational Books 245 Grandview, Laguna Beach, California 92651

Instant Words 986-1005

corn	seat
substances	division
smell	effect
tools	underline
conditions	view
cows	afternoon
track	national
arrived	salt
located	replace
sir	dots

Word Study   Phonogram "-ot"

dots	hot	pot
hot	shot	got

Note: There are 2 compound words in this list: "afternoon" and "underline".

Variant forms

corned	cow
sirs	divisions
substance	afternoons
smelled smellers smelling smells	tool tooled tooling
condition conditioned conditioning	tracked trackers
arrive arrives arriving	tracking tracks
locate locates locating	seated seating seats
effected effecting effects	underlined underlining
viewed viewing views	nationally nationals
salted salting salts	replaceable replaced
dot dotted dotting	replaces replacing

Review: Selected Instant Words in Lessons 71, 72, & 73.

Laguna Beach Educational Books 245 Grandview, Laguna Beach, California 92651

Instant Words 1006-1025

chair	**press**
chord	**range**
segment	**season**
sheet	**spend**
camp	**proper**
composer	**silver**
dream	**glad**
protect	**leader**
bar	**atoms**
band	**guide**

Word Study   Phonogram "-amp"

camp	**damp**	**tramp**
lamp	**champ**	**stamp**

Note: The long /ē/ sound is spelled "ea" in 3 of these words: "dream", "leader", and "season", and spelled "ee" in "sheet".

Variant forms

chairs
composers
properly
segmented segments
dreamed dreamer dreamers
dreaming dreamless dreams
barred barring bars
ranged ranges ranging
seasoned seasons
silvered silvering
leaders
guided guides guiding

sheets
bands
chording chords
camped camping camps
protected protecting
protects
pressed presser
presses pressing
spending spends
gladdest gladly gladness
atom

Review: Word Study in Lessons 72, 73, & 74.

Laguna Beach Educational Books 245 Grandview, Laguna Beach, California 92651

Instant Words 1026-1045

mass	parents
shore	multiply
anyone	required
busy	degrees
replied	gray
weigh	railroad
share	double
charge	thank
original	coat
drink	feed

Word Study   Phonogram "-ink"

drink	blink	think
sink	pink	stink

Note: There are 4 words with a silent "e" at the end: "shore", "anyone", "charge", "double". You will note that, while "e" is usually silent at the end of a word that contains another vowel, the final "e" doesn't always make the preceding vowel long.

Variant forms

massed masses massing	shores
parent	degree
busied busier busiest busily	replies reply replying
weighed weighing weights	shared shares sharing
charged charges charging	originally originals
drinker drinkers drinking drinks	multiplied multiplies
require requires requiring	multiplying
grayed graying grays	railroaders railroading
doubled doubles doubling	railroads
thanked thanking thanks	coated costs
feeding feeds	

Review: Check Personal Spelling Lists. Partners quiz on each other's Personal Spelling Lists.

Laguna Beach Educational Books 245 Grandview, Laguna Beach, California 92651

Instant Words 1046-1065

service	station
market	enemy
teeth	plate
mixed	I'd
meant	spoke
quotient	bread
combined	dear
support	speech
gathered	ancient
pressure	liquid

Word Study   Phonics: Short "e" and long "e" spelled "ea"

Short /ĕ/	Long /ē/
bread	deal dream
meant	seat season
death	leader dear

Note: Caution - "ea" makes either a short /ĕ/ sound or a long /ē/ sound.

Variant forms

services	marketed marketing
mix mixes mixing	markets
quotients	combine combines
supported supporting supports	combining
gather gatherers gathers	pressured pressures
stationed stations	pressuring
enemies	speeches
liquids	plated plates plating
spokes	breads
dearer dearest dearly dears	anciently ancients

Review: Selected Instant Words in Lessons 74, 75, & 76.

Laguna Beach Educational Books 245 Grandview, Laguna Beach, California 92651

Instant Words 1066-1085

removed	log
basic	spent
climate	community
chemical	wagon
skill	bag
chapter	manufacturing
you'll	cup
kitchen	model
minerals	signal
occur	noise

Word Study   Spelling Pattern: Double "ll" (final)

Double "ll"	Single "l"
skill will	chemical model
you'll smell	mineral signal

Note: Watch out for the final "l". Sometimes it is doubled and sometimes it is single.

Variant forms

remove   removes   removing   climates
chemically   chemicals   skilled   skills
chapters   kitchens
mineral   occurred   occurring
logged   logger   loggers   logging   logs   occurs
communities   wagons
bagged   bags   manufacture manufactured
cupped   cupping   cups   manufacturers
modeled   modeling   models   signaled   signaling
noises   signals

Review: Word Study in Lessons 75, 76, & 77.

Laguna Beach Educational Books 245 Grandview, Laguna Beach, California 92651

Instant Words 1086-1105

multiplication	shining
court	purpose
path	loan
composition	nature
continent	prove
fat	newspaper
promised	tune
handle	grown
smooth	angry
shells	breathe

Word Study   Phonics: Long "o" spelled "oa" and "ow"

<u>Spelled "oa"</u>   <u>Spelled "ow"</u>
load   coast   grown   know
coat   boat   own   flow

Note: The long /ō/ sound can be spelled either "oa" or "ow".

Variant forms

multiplications
paths
continents
promise   promises   promising
smoothed   smoother   smoothest
smoothing   smoothly   smoothness   smooths
purposed   purposely   purposes
natures
newspapers
tuned   tunes   tuning
breathable   breathed   breathes   breathing

courted   courting   courts
compositions
fats   fatter   fattest
handled   handles   handling
shell   shelled   shelling
shine   shined   shines
loaded   loaders
loading   loads
proved   proven
angrier   angrily

Review: Check Personal Spelling List. Partners quiz.

Laguna Beach Educational Books 245 Grandview, Laguna Beach, California 92651

Instant Words 1106-1125

depends	proud
attack	nest
hurt	colonies
narrow	digits
muscles	grandfather
therefore	sort
cap	master
motion	layer
population	player
vegetables	beyond

Word Study   Spelling Pattern "-ayer"

layer	sprayer	sayer
player	payer	strayer

Note: For just the "ay" digraph making the long /ā/ sound, see Lesson 16.

Variant forms

depend   depended
hurting   hurts
narrowed   narrower   narrowest
narrowing   narrowly   narrowness   narrows
motioned   motioning   motions
vegetable
nested   nesting   nests
digit
sorted   sorting   sorts
layered   layers
players

attacked   attackers
attacking   attacks
muscle
capped   caps
populations
prouder proudest proudly
colony
grandfathers
mastered mastering
masters

Review: Selected Instant Words in Lessons 77, 78, & 79.

Laguna Beach Educational Books 245 Grandview, Laguna Beach, California 92651

Instant Words 1126-1145

trail	rays
events	shot
public	sold
grain	topic
rate	attention
rushed	musical
thread	pour
what's	Spanish
offered	suit
union	strike

Word Study   Phonogram "-ail"

trail	sail	fail
nail	tail	jail

Note: The digraph "ai" usually makes the long /ā/ sound. See Lesson 47.

Variant forms

trailed trailing trails
publicity
rated rates rating
threaded threading threads
unionism unions
shots
attentions
poured pouring pours
striker strikes striking

event
grains
rush rushes rushing
offer offers
ray
topics
musicals
suited suiting suits

Review: Word Study in Lessons 78, 79, & 80.

Laguna Beach Educational Books 245 Grandview, Laguna Beach, California 92651

Instant Words 1146-1165

arranged	sad
cabin	snake
imagine	average
storm	Christmas
whale	hide
ant	variety
central	airplane
sheep	chicken
tired	bottle
program	coal

Word Study   Phonics: Final "l" spelled "l" and "le"

<u>Spelled "le"</u>   <u>Spelled "l"</u>
whale   muscle   coal   trail
bottle   triangle   central   model

Note: The final /l/ or /el/ sound is spelled a number of ways. See the single "l" in "coal" and "le" in "bottle". For the final /l/ sound spelled "ll", see Lesson 78.

Variant forms

arrange   arranger   arrangers   arranging   cabins
imagined   imagines   imagining   imaginings   stormed   storming   storms
whales   whaling   ants
tiredly   tiredness   programmed   programming
sadder   saddest   sadly   sadness   programs
snaked   snakes   averaged   averages
hiders   hides   hiding   averaging
varieties   airplanes
chickens   bottled   bottles
coals

Review: Check Personal Spelling List. Partners quiz.

Laguna Beach Educational Books 245 Grandview, Laguna Beach, California 92651

Instant Words 1166-1185

myself	**throughout**
solid	**recent**
source	**bat**
alike	**graph**
dishes	**Roman**
rabbit	**throw**
gently	**folk**
collect	**strip**
mama	**structure**
rapidly	**apply**

Word Study   Phonics "f" sound spelled "ph"

graph	**phonics**	**alphabet**
phrase	**phone**	**photograph**

Note: Not too often, but sometimes, the /f/ sound is spelled "ph".

Variant forms

solidly   solids
dish
gentle   gentled   gentleness   gentler
rapid   rapids
recently
graphed   graphing   graphs
thrower   throwing   throws
stripped   stripping   strips
applied   applies   applying

sources
rabbits
collected   collecting
collects
bats   batted   batting
Romans
folks
structures

Review: Selected Instant Words in Lessons 80, 81, & 82.

Laguna Beach Educational Books 245 Grandview, Laguna Beach, California 92651

Instant Words 1186-1205

regular	search
dinner	lose
activities	pencil
Latin	useful
nice	won
according	worry
realized	giant
related	wonderful
recognize	cloth
refer	farther

Word Study   Phonogram "-ice"

nice	price	slice
rice	twice	lice

Note: This phonogram conforms to the Final "e" Rule, which states that "e" at the end of a word makes the preceding vowel long and the "e" is silent.

Variant forms

regularly   regulars
activity
nicer   nicest
realize   realizes   realizing
relate   relates   relating
referred   referring   refers
loser   losers   loses   losing
penciled   pencils
worried   worries   worrying
cloths

dinners
Latins
accord   accorded
accordingly
recognized   recognizing
searched   searchers
searches   searching
usefulness
giants
wonderfully
wonderfulness

Review: Word Study in Lessons 81, 82, & 83.

Laguna Beach Educational Books 245 Grandview, Laguna Beach, California 92651

Instant Words 1206-1225

hanging	battle
California	style
pack	bridge
article	connected
subtract	beauty
wet	driver
ate	meal
electricity	melted
taste	met
height	stage

Word Study   Phonogram "-eal"

meal	seal	heal
real	steal	deal

Note: Two of these phonogram words have homophones. "Heel" means back of foot and "heal" means to cure. "Steal" means to take unlawfully and "steel" is a metal.

Variant forms

hang   hanged   hangs
packed   packing   packs
subtracted   subtracting   subtracts
tasted   tastes   tasting
heights
styled   styles   styling
bridged   bridges   bridging
drivers
meals
melt   melting   melts

Californian Californians
articles
wetness   wetted   wetter
wettest   wetting
battled   battler
battles   battling
connect   connecting
connector connectors
connects
staged   stages   staging

Review: Check Personal Spelling Lists. Partners quiz.

Laguna Beach Educational Books 245 Grandview, Laguna Beach, California 92651

Instant Words 1226-1245

aunt	German
feathers	herself
price	Mexico
queen	Russia
hall	empty
lion	expression
nine	neighbors
review	fence
bowl	automobile
development	card

Word Study   Phonogram "-ard"

card	guard	lard
yard	hard	bard

Note: Just the "ar" sound was in Lesson 33.

Variant forms

aunts   aunty
priced   prices
halls
nines
bowled   bowling   bowls
developmental   developments
Germans
emptied   empties   emptiness   emptying
neighbor
automobiles

feather   feathered
queenly   queens
lions
reviewed   reviewer
reviewers   reviewing
reviews
Russian   Russians
expressions
fenced   fences   fencing
cards

Review: Selected Instant Words in Lessons 83, 84, & 85.

Laguna Beach Educational Books 245 Grandview, Laguna Beach, California 92651

Instant Words 1246-1265

danger	till
engineer	beach
lesson	forgot
obtain	rode
discuss	knowledge
fourth	shade
function	shadow
performed	brave
piano	indeed
Asia	lord

Word Study   Phonics: Long "o" spelled "o" and "ow"

<u>Spelled "o"</u>   <u>Spelled "ow"</u>
piano no   shadow   throw
go so   know   blow

Note: The final long /ō/ sound can be spelled either "ow" or "o". Unfortunately the letters "ow" also make the /ou/ sound as in "how". The "ow" in "knowledge" is an exception (it's a short /o/).

Variant forms

dangers   lessons
fourth   pianos
forgotten   engineered engineering
obtainable obtained obtaining obtains   engineers
discussed discusses discussing   functioning functions
perform performing performs   Asian Asians
tilled tilling   beached beaches
shaded shades shading   shadowed shadowing
braved bravely braver braves lords
bravest braving

Review: Word Study in Lessons 84, 85, & 86.

Laguna Beach Educational Books 245 Grandview, Laguna Beach, California 92651

Instant Words 1266-1285

Negro	**slipped**
pronounce	**curve**
stared	**frame**
we're	**shook**
pitch	**writer**
dad	**freedom**
duck	**slightly**
fixed	**television**
hungry	**blank**
operation	**cowboy**

Word Study   Phonogram "-ame"

frame	**game**	**same**
came	**name**	**shame**

Note: This phonogram conforms to the Final "e" Rule.

Variant forms

Negroes
stare stares staring
pitched pitches pitching
fix fixes fixing
operations
curved curves curving curvy
writers
slight slightest
cowboys

pronounced pronounces
pronouncing
ducked ducking ducks
hungrier hungrily
slip slipping
framed frames framing
freedoms
blanked blankly blanks

Review: Check Personal Spelling Lists. Partners quiz.

Laguna Beach Educational Books 245 Grandview, Laguna Beach, California 92651

Instant Words 1286-1305

eastern	neck
message	pocket
apart	clock
judge	simply
smoke	steam
bus	fold
disease	title
flights	escape
brush	extend
forth	sweet

Word Study   Phonogram "-eet"

sweet	street	sheet
greet	meet	beet

Note: 2 of these phonogram words are homophones. "Beet" is a vegetable and "beat" means to conquer. "Meet" means to come together and "meat" is a food.

Variant forms

messages
smoked   smokes   smoking
brushed   brushes   brushing
pocketed   pockets
steamed   steaming
titled   titles
extended   extending   extends

judged   judges   judging
buses
necks
clocked   clocks
folded   folding   folds
escaped   escapes   escaping
sweeter   sweetest   sweetly
sweetness   sweets

Review: Selected Instant Words in Lessons 86, 87, & 88.

Laguna Beach Educational Books 245 Grandview, Laguna Beach, California 92651

Instant Words 1306-1325

teach	neither
tears	popular
club	twenty
tight	gain
arrow	onto
barn	quarter
familiar	spider
none	unless
flew	atmosphere
trap	diagram

Word Study   Phonogram "-each"

teach	peach	preach
reach	beach	bleach

Note: The digraph "ea" making the long /ē/ sound is in Lesson 32, and the digraph "ch" was in Lesson 46.

Variant forms

teaches   teaching
clubs
arrows
trapped   trapper   trappers
trapping   traps
gained   gaining   gains
spiders
diagrammed   diagramming   diagrams

tear   tearing
tighter   tightly   tights
barns
popularly
twenties
quartered   quarters
atmospheres

Review: Word Study in Lessons 87, 88, & 89.

Laguna Beach Educational Books 245 Grandview, Laguna Beach, California 92651

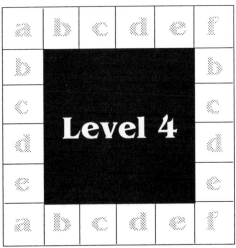

Level 4

Lessons 91-125

This Section contains 35 Lessons
Each Lesson contains:

- **20 Spelling Words**
    Instant Words Ranks 1326-2025

- **Word Study**
    phonics, spelling rules, blends, phonograms, homophones, etc.

- **Variant Forms**
    of the Instant Words in the Lesson

- **Review suggestions**

Instant Words 1326-1345

Texas	hurry
twice	jar
Atlantic	funny
character	secret
breakfast	concerned
hunters	slaves
potatoes	everybody
prime	Pacific
project	paid
rocket	creatures

Word Study   Spelling Rule: Plurals and "s" form

1. For most words, just add an "s" to make it plural:

    rocket-rockets   jar-jars   slave-slaves

2. For words ending in "y", change "y" to "i" and add "es".

    funny-funnies   hurry-hurries

Variant forms

characters
hunter
primes priming
rocketed rocketing rockets
hurries hurrying
funnier funniest
concern concerning concerns
creature

breakfasts
potato
projected projecting
projects
jarred jarring jars
secretly secrets
slave slaving

Review: Start students keeping a Personal Spelling List, see Appendix 4 for suggestions.

Laguna Beach Educational Books 245 Grandview, Laguna Beach, California 92651

Instant Words 1346-1365

roar	pipe
fellow	congress
settlers	peace
breath	Egypt
cake	gate
consists	mount
rod	dust
whispered	established
mills	officer
penny	brain

Word Study   Phonics: Blend "br"

brain	breath	branches
brush	breathe	brown

Note: Consonant blends retain the sound of both consonants blended together.

Variant forms

roared   roaring   roars
settler
caked   cakes
rods
whisper   whispering   whispers
pennies
congresses
gates
dusted   dusting   dusts
establish   establishes   establishing
brains

fellows
breaths
consist   consisted
consisting
mill   milling
piped   pipes   piping
Egyptian   Egyptians
mounted   mounting
mounts
officers

Review: Most of the major phonics rules are covered in the Phonics sections of Lessons 1-55. The Chart in Appendix 7 gives a more complete phonics skills listing.

Laguna Beach Educational Books 245 Grandview, Laguna Beach, California 92651

Instant Words 1366-1385

pond	tip
serious	alive
lunch	approached
steady	post
carbon	elephant
floating	disappeared
improve	ranch
manner	golden
political	parallel
scientific	estimate

Word Study   Phonics: Blend "st"

steady	stop	estimate
stand	post	fast

Variant forms

ponds	lunches
carbons	seriously seriousness
steadied steadier steadily	float floated floats
steadiness steadying	improved improves
mannered manners	improving
politically	scientifically
tipped tipping tips	approach approaches
posted posting posts	approaching
elephants	disappear disappearing
ranches ranching	disappears
gold	paralleled parallels
estimated estimates estimating	

Review: Look over the Phonogram chart in Appendix 8. It can be helpful in explaining or relating new words.

Laguna Beach Educational Books 245 Grandview, Laguna Beach, California 92651

Instant Words 1386-1405

firmly	**cave**
rough	**quality**
examine	**select**
involved	**tribes**
explore	**wooden**
laid	**China**
artist	**powerful**
drew	**horn**
scene	**standard**
Alaska	**future**

Word Study   Homophones

scene = part of a play or place where something happens ("the scene of an accident")

seen = past form of the verb "to see" ("He was seen at school.")

Variant forms

firm   firmer   firmness   firms
examined   examiner   examiners
examines   examining
explored   explores   exploring
artists
Alaskan   Alaskans
qualities
tribe
horns
futures

rougher   roughing
roughly   roughness
involve   involvement
involves   involving
scenes
caved   caves   caving
selected   selecting
powerfully
standards

Review: Selected Instant Words in Lessons 91, 92, & 93. It will be suggested that you review the Instant Words in the preceding 3 Lessons every 3rd Lesson.

Laguna Beach Educational Books 245 Grandview, Laguna Beach, California 92651

Instant Words 1406-1425

accent	relative
identify	spirit
individual	strength
whom	button
accept	library
clay	pile
date	shoot
tomorrow	papa
desk	affect
drove	immediately

Word Study   Spelling Pattern: Double consonants
Double consonants often occur when the same sound ends one syllable and begins the next one.

ac cent   to mor row   but ton
ac cept   im me di ate ly

Variant forms

accented   accenting   accents   identified   identifies
individuals   identifying
accepted   accepting   accepts   clays
dated   dates   dating   desks
relatively   relatives   spirited   spirits
strengths   libraries
immediate   buttoned   buttoning
piled   piles   piling   buttons
shooter   shooters   affected   affecting
shooting   shootings   affects

Review: Word Study in Lessons 91, 92, 93, & 94.

Laguna Beach Educational Books 245 Grandview, Laguna Beach, California 92651

Instant Words 1426-1445

nails	magnet
pan	rhyme
balance	upper
college	vote
orchestra	ruler
bend	telephone
forget	fur
warning	satellites
orbit	health
highway	principle

Word Study   Homophones

principle = a rule or basic trust; "principle of law"

principal = head of a school staff, chief person, money on which interest is paid; "principal of a school"; "principal and interest"

Variant forms

nail nailed nailing
balanced balances balancing
orchestral orchestras
forgets forgettable forgetting
orbital orbited orbiter
orbiting orbits
magnets
uppers
furs
telephoned telephones
telephoning

panned pans
colleges
bending bends
warn warned
warning warns
highways
rhymed rhymes rhyming
rulers
voted votes voting
satellite
principles

Review: Check to make sure each student is keeping a Personal Spelling List. See Appendix 5 for suggestions on Personal Spelling Lists. Partners can quiz each other on Personal Spelling Lists.

Laguna Beach Educational Books 245 Grandview, Laguna Beach, California 92651

Instant Words 1446-1465

particles	drum
roof	equivalent
tax	reader
Italy	rubber
swing	surrounded
wise	they're
citizens	university
daughter	basket
pigs	drawn
vary	effort

Word Study   Phonics: Blend "dr"

drum	drive	drop
drawn	drink	dress

Variant forms

particle	roofed roofing roofs
taxed taxes	swinging swings
wisely wiser wisest	citizen
daughters	pig
varied varies varying	drummed drumming
equivalents	drums
readers	rubbers
surround surrounding surrounds	universities
baskets	efforts

Review: Selected Instant Words in Lessons 94, 95, & 96.

Laguna Beach Educational Books 245 Grandview, Laguna Beach, California 92651

Instant Words 1466-1485

multiples	**characteristics**
series	**copper**
wheat	**guard**
Chinese	**hidden**
discovery	**balloon**
puzzle	**baseball**
twelve	**bow**
influence	**nobody**
threw	**waste**
trick	**learned**

Word Study   Phonics: "k" sound spelled "ch"

characteristics	**Christmas**	**chord**
chorus	**chemistry**	**character**

Note: Usually "ch" makes the /ch/ sound heard in "child". See Lesson 46.

Variant forms

multiple
puzzled puzzles puzzling
tricked tricks
characteristic characteristically
guarded guarding guards
ballooned ballooning balloons
bowing bows
lean leaner leaning leans

discoveries
influenced influences
influencing
coppers
hid
baseballs
wasted wastes wasting

Review: Word Study in Lessons 95, 96, & 97.

Laguna Beach Educational Books 245 Grandview, Laguna Beach, California 92651

Instant Words 1486-1505

theory	dozen
tongue	nearby
friendly	orange
struggle	vast
crack	combination
Germany	pie
invented	rational
prevent	sick
broad	worth
denominator	growth

Word Study   Phonics: Blend "gr"

growth	grew	graph
gray	ground	grass

Variant forms

theories	tongued tongues
friendliest friendliness	cracked cracking
struggled struggles struggling	cracks
invent inventing invents	broader broadest
prevented preventing prevents	broadly
denominators	oranges
dozens	combinations
vastly vastness	rationally
pies	growths

Review: Check Personal Spelling List. Partners quiz.

Laguna Beach Educational Books 245 Grandview, Laguna Beach, California 92651

Instant Words 1506-1525

bushes	expanded
deer	fabric
flag	fifty
married	mud
stock	shaking
dinosaurs	further
instance	slope
limited	dig
pony	mistakes
volume	official

Word Study   Homophones

deer = an animal   marry = join together

dear = much loved   Mary = girl's name
      or valued

                  merry = happy, laughing

Variant forms

bush   flagged   flags
marries   marry   dinosaur
instances   limit   limiting
ponies   limitless   limits
expand   expanding   expands   fabrics
fifties   fiftieth   shake   shakes
furthering   sloped   slopes   sloping
digger   diggers   mistake   mistaking
digging   diggings   officially   officials

Review: Selected Instant Words in Lessons 97, 98, & 99.

Laguna Beach Educational Books 245 Grandview, Laguna Beach, California 92651

Instant Words 1526-1545

tower	cream
slide	dangerous
Spain	hung
supper	pronunciation
bake	education
frightened	failed
zero	favorite
terrible	items
bees	plenty
beneath	wore

Word Study   Phonogram "-ung"

hung	stung	swung
sung	lung	flung

Variant forms

towered   towering   towers
suppers
baked   baking   bakes
zeroed   zeroing   zeros
bee
dangerously
pronunciations
fail   failing
failings   fails

slider   sliders
slides   sliding
frighten   frightens
terribly
creamed   creaming
creams
educations
favorites
item

Review: Word Study in Lessons 98, 99, & 100.

Laguna Beach Educational Books 245 Grandview, Laguna Beach, California 92651

Instant Words 1546-1565

attempt	**sports**
avoid	**stems**
pleasant	**you've**
rubbed	**destroyed**
stamp	**frog**
stir	**measurement**
blanket	**situation**
knife	**composed**
prince	**herd**
exist	**needle**

Word Study   Phonics: "oi"

avoid	**oil**	**noise**
join	**voice**	**boil**

Note: The letters "oi" make the same diphthong sound as /oy/ in "boy". Watch out for the silent "k" in "knife".

Variant forms

attempted attempting attempts
pleasantly
stamped stamping stamps
blanketed blanketing blankets
existed existing exists
stem stemmed stemming
frogs
measurements
compose composes composing
needled needles

avoided avoiding avoids
rub rubbing rubs
stirred stirring stirs
princes
sport sported sporting
destroy destroying
destroys
situations
herded herding herds

Review: Check Personal Spelling Lists. Partners quiz.

Laguna Beach Educational Books 245 Grandview, Laguna Beach, California 92651

Instant Words 1566-1585

spin	fastened
organized	advance
poet	canal
bay	coins
hurried	label
illustrate	butter
pet	everywhere
route	local
unusual	pa
crew	whistle

Word Study   Phonics: Blend "sp"

spin	speech	Spanish
special	spell	sports

Note: Watch out for the silent "t" in "whistle" and "fastened".

Variant forms

spinner spinners
spinning spins
poets
hurriedly
pets petted petting
routed router routes
crews
advanced advances advancing
coin coined coining
buttered buttering buttery
whistled whistles whistling

organize organizers
organizes organizing
bays
illustrated illustrates
illustrating
unusually
fasten fastens
canals
labeled labeling labels
locally locals

Review: Selected Instant Words in Lessons 100, 101, & 102.

Laguna Beach Educational Books 245 Grandview, Laguna Beach, California 92651

Instant Words 1586-1605

honor	journey
knees	lungs
successful	yelled
whatever	environment
fox	fuel
globe	gift
pin	buffalo
pronoun	equipment
candy	Italian
India	earn

Word Study   Phonogram "-ift"

gift	swift	thrift
lift	sift	shift

Note: The final /ks/ sound spelled "x" in "fox", also in "box" and "lox", Lesson 71. The same final /ks/ sound is spelled "cks" in "locks" and "blocks".

Variant forms

honored honoring honors	knee
successfully	foxes
globes	pinned pinning pins
pronouns	candied candies
journeyed journeying journeys	lung
yell yelling	environments
fuels	gifts
buffaloes	Italians
earned earners earning earns	

Review: Word Study in Lessons 101, 102, & 103.

Laguna Beach Educational Books 245 Grandview, Laguna Beach, California 92651

Instant Words 1606-1625

kids	fort
visitors	demand
glance	leaped
sailors	lips
adverb	motor
beans	shut
desired	claim
prefix	lovely
society	wound
eager	asleep

Word Study   Phonics: schwa "a"

asleep	ago	ahead
about	afraid	alone

Note: The beginning letter "a" makes a schwa /ə/ sound when it forms a separate unaccented syllable. For example, "asleep". The "a" in "adverb" is not a schwa because the syllable is "ad".

Variant forms

kid kidding	visitor
glanced glances glancing	sailor
adverbs	bean
desire desires desiring	prefixes
societies	eagerly eagerness
forts	demanded demanding
leap leaping leaps	demands
lip	motoring motors
shuts shutting	claimed claiming claims
loveliest loveliness	wounded wounding
	wounds

Review: Check Personal Spelling Lists. Partners quiz.

Laguna Beach Educational Books 245 Grandview, Laguna Beach, California 92651

Instant Words 1626-1645

blend	bark
magic	constant
native	frequently
nodded	port
tent	reflected
boiling	extra
fractional	social
habits	swift
lack	adventure
treated	personal

Word Study   Phonogram "-ent"

tent	cent	spent
bent	rent	scent

Note: "cent" and "scent" are homophones.

Variant forms

blended blending blends	natives
nod nodding nods	tents
boil boiled boils	habit
lacked lacking lacks	treat treating treats
barking barks	constantly constants
frequent frequented	ports
reflect reflecting reflects	extras
swifter swiftest swiftly	adventures adventuring
swiftness swifts	personally

Review: Selected Instant Words in Lessons 103, 104, & 105.

Laguna Beach Educational Books 245 Grandview, Laguna Beach, California 92651

Instant Words 1646-1665

prize	coffee
sunlight	castle
bare	hadn't
lock	knocked
thee	merely
belt	physical
chain	stroke
features	ability
harbor	device
tank	owner

Word Study   Phonics: final "ee"

thee	see	three
coffee	knee	fee

Note: The long /ē/ sound is sometimes spelled "ee", but more often it is spelled "y" as in "merely" or "ability". However, a few older dictionaries would say that the final "y" in "merely" would be a short /i/.

Variant forms

prized prizes	bared barely
locked locking locks	belted belting belts
chained chains	feature featured
harbored harboring harbors	featureless featuring
tanks	castles
knock knocking knocks	mere
physically	stroked strokes stroking
abilities	devices
owners	

Review: Word Study in Lessons 104, 105, & 106.

Laguna Beach Educational Books 245 Grandview, Laguna Beach, California 92651

Instant Words 1666-1685

taught	**mirror**
weak	**outline**
federal	**deck**
ordinary	**police**
sorry	**species**
cage	**stranger**
joy	**electrons**
monkey	**foreign**
odd	**fought**
account	**industrial**

Word Study   Spelling Pattern "ought"

fought	**thought**	**taught**
bought	**ought**	**caught**

Note: This is a difficult Spelling Pattern we inherited from Old English. The sound /ôt/ is usually spelled "ought", but in a very few words it is spelled "aught", mainly "taught" and "caught".

Variant forms

weaker   weakest
caged   cages
monkeys
accounted   accounts
outlined   outlines   outlining
strangers
industrially

federally   federals
joys
odder   oddest   oddly
mirrored   mirrors
decked   decking   decks
electron

Review: Check Personal Spelling Lists. Partners quiz.

Laguna Beach Educational Books 245 Grandview, Laguna Beach, California 92651

Instant Words 1686-1705

accident	twisted
department	lying
flash	mixture
whenever	remind
grade	reptiles
invited	captured
pioneers	flame
predicate	flood
stitch	jet
turkey	loose

Word Study   Phonics: Blend "fl"

flash	flood	fly
flame	flowers	flight

Note: Watch out for the final /s/ sound, which is spelled 3 different ways in this Lesson: "se" in "loose", "es" in "reptiles", and "s" in "pioneers".

Variant forms

accidents	departments
flashed flashes flashing	graded grades grading
invite invites inviting	pioneer pioneered
predicates	pioneering
turkeys	mixtures
stitched stitches stitching	twist twisting twists
reminded reminder reminders	reptile
reminding reminds	capture captures
flamed flames flaming	capturing
flooded flooding floods	jets jetted
loosed loosely	

Review: Selected Instant Words in Lessons 106, 107, & 108.

Laguna Beach Educational Books 245 Grandview, Laguna Beach, California 92651

Instant Words 1706-1725

rice	mold
differ	theme
diving	blind
grinned	attached
package	mighty
pool	resources
contrast	tickets
managed	doubt
Canada	pilot
diameter	pupils

Word Study   Phonics: Open and Closed Syllables

Short /i/   dif fer   **Long /ī/**   di ving

Closed Syllable   grin ned   **Open Syllable**   mi ghty

                     tick ets   pi lot

Note: Open Syllables (syllable ends with vowel) tend to have long vowel sounds and Closed Syllables (syllable ends with a consonant) tend to have the short vowel sound. But not always.
Example: "blind" and "pupils".

Variant forms

differed differing differs	dive dived dives
grin grinning grins	packaged packages
pooling pools	packaging
contrasted contrasting contrasts	manage managing
diameters	moldable molded
themes	molding molds
pupil	blind blinding blindingly
attach attaches attaching	blindly blindness blinds
mightier mighties	resource
mightiest mightily	ticket
doubted doubters doubting doubt	piloted piloting pilots

Review: Word Study in Lessons 107, 108, & 109.

Laguna Beach Educational Books 245 Grandview, Laguna Beach, California 92651

Instant Words 1726-1745

silence	trunk
tide	author
birthday	outer
medicine	pump
sang	sung
construction	tossed
perfect	valuable
gradually	adult
progress	appearance
specific	chest

Word Study   Phonics: Blend "pr"

progress	prime	principle
practice	princess	printed

Note: The changed past forms for "sing" in this Lesson: "sang" and "sung".

Variant forms

silenced silences	tides
birthdays	medicines
constructional constructions	perfected perfecting
gradual	progressed progresses
specifically	progressing
trunks	authors
pumped pumpers pumping pumps	toss tosses tossing
valuables	adults
appearances	chests

Review: Check Personal Spelling Lists. Partners quiz.

Laguna Beach Educational Books 245 Grandview, Laguna Beach, California 92651

Instant Words 1746-1765

sale	Paris
sample	swallowed
wrapped	telescope
introduced	thou
mentioned	definition
passengers	grabbed
shirt	grant
choice	aid
crawled	excitement
meter	husband

Word Study   Grammar: Capitalize proper nouns

Paris	Germany	China
Mary	Chinese	Alaska

Note: Proper nouns are specific names for persons, places and things - all are capitalized.

Variant forms

sales   sampled   samples
wrap   wrapping   wraps   sampling   samplings
introduce   introduces   introducing   mention   mentioning
passenger   mentions
shirts   choices
crawl   crawling   crawls   crawly   meters
swallow   swallowing   swallows   telescopes   telescoping
definitional   definitions   grab   grabbing   grabs
granted   granting   grants   aided   aiding   aids
husbands

Review: Selected Instant Words in Lessons 109, 110, & 111.

Laguna Beach Educational Books 245 Grandview, Laguna Beach, California 92651

Instant Words 1766-1785

research	safety
respect	scratch
border	success
cheese	turtle
bite	yesterday
Boston	candle
gravity	darkness
link	guests
normal	operate
refused	crystals

Word Study   Phonogram "-ite"

bite	white	quite
kite	write	spite

Note: This phonogram follows the Final "e" Rule. It also was the same sound /ī/ as the "-ight" phonogram in Lesson 31.

Variant forms

researched   researcher   researchers   respected   respecting
researches   researching   respects
bordered   bordering   borders   cheeses
bites   biting   Bostonians
linkage   linked   linking   links   normally
refuse   refuses   refusing   scratched   scratches
successes   scratching
turtles   candles
guest   operated   operates
crystal   operating

Review: Word Study in Lessons 110, 111, & 112.

Laguna Beach Educational Books 245 Grandview, Laguna Beach, California 92651

Instant Words 1786-1805

hammer	toes
o'clock	vertical
passage	depth
wool	exclaimed
hook	jungle
London	minor
mail	mood
opinion	daily
organization	movie
construct	pot

Word Study   Phonics: "oo" Long and Short

Short /o͝o/   **Long /o͞o/**
wool   flood   mood   loose
hook   look   pool   moon

Note: The digraph "oo" has both a long and short sound and there is no rule to tell you when to use either sound. The letter "u" can make either of these sounds, for example, "truth" and "put".

Variant forms

hammered hammering hammers   passages
hooked hooking hooks   mailed mailing
opinions   mailings mails
organizational organizations   constructed constructing
toe   constructs
vertically   depths
exclaim exclaiming exclaims   jungles
minors   moods
movies   pots potted

Review: Check Personal Spelling Lists. Partners quiz.

Laguna Beach Educational Books 245 Grandview, Laguna Beach, California 92651

Instant Words 1806-1825

satisfied	wandering
heading	clues
practical	customs
burst	dragged
fifth	drill
mouse	camera
negative	equator
she's	extremely
tales	sighed
toy	singular

Word Study   Phonics: "oy"

toy	enjoy	royal
boy	loyal	soy

Note: The /oy/ sound can also be spelled "oi" as in "oil".

Variant forms

satisfies satisfy satisfying
practically
fifths
tale
wander wandered wanderer
wanderers wanderings
drag dragging drags
cameras
extreme extremes
singularly singulars

headings
bursting bursts
negatively negatives
toys
clue
custom
drilled driller
drilling drills
sign sighing signs

Review: Selected Instant Words in Lessons 112, 113, & 114.

Laguna Beach Educational Books 245 Grandview, Laguna Beach, California 92651

Instant Words 1826-1845

straw	bent
vessels	chase
mammals	conversation
pop	revolution
task	traffic
pine	Virginia
subtraction	collection
territory	mission
accurate	nerve
Australia	troops

Word Study   Spelling Pattern "tion"

subtrac<u>tion</u>	conversa<u>tion</u>
collec<u>tion</u>	mis<u>sion</u>

Note: Most of the time the ending /sh∂n/ sound is spelled "tion", but occasionally it is spelled "sion" as in "mission".

Variant forms

straws	vessel
mammal mammalian	popped popping pops
tasks	pines
subtractions	territories
accurately	Australian Australians
chased chases chasing	conversations
revolutions	Virginian Virginians
collections	missions
nerved nerves	troop trooped trooping

Review: Word Study in Lessons 113, 114, & 115.

Laguna Beach Educational Books 245 Grandview, Laguna Beach, California 92651

Instant Words 1846-1865

Mississippi	dare
celebrate	Dutch
circus	kick
joint	lonely
misspelled	net
setting	notation
you'd	Saturday
available	tea
bicycle	trace
boots	aren't

Word Study   Phonogram "-ace"

trace	face	space
place	race	lace

Note: This phonogram follows the Final "e" Rule. Watch out for the 2 contractions "aren't" and "you'd".

Variant forms

celebrated celebrates celebrating
celebration celebrations
misspell misspelling
misspellings misspells
boot
kicked kicking kicks
lonelier loneliness
Saturdays

circuses
jointed joints
settings
bicycles bicycling
dared dares
daring daringly
nets netted netting
traced traces

Review: Check Personal Spelling Lists. Partners quiz.

Laguna Beach Educational Books 245 Grandview, Laguna Beach, California 92651

Instant Words 1866-1885

audience	released
evidence	we've
principal	attracted
production	constitution
united	delight
bound	frozen
Chicago	haven't
curious	powder
dam	pretend
goat	princess

Word Study   Phonics: Broad ô sound spelled "au"

<u>au</u>dience	<u>au</u>tomobile	bec<u>au</u>se
<u>Au</u>stralia	<u>au</u>thor	d<u>au</u>ghter

Note: Occasionally the broad /ô/ sound is spelled "a" as in "want".

Variant forms

audiences	evidenced evidences
principally principals	productions
unite uniting	bounded bounding
Chicagoan	bounds
curiously	dammed dams
goats	froze
release releases releasing	attract attracting
constitutions	attracts
delighted delightedly	powdered powders
delighting delights	pretended pretending
princesses	pretends

Review: Selected Instant Words in Lessons 115, 116, & 117.

Laguna Beach Educational Books 245 Grandview, Laguna Beach, California 92651

Instant Words 1886-1905

relationship	pasture
beam	pen
borrowed	recording
explorers	selection
grandmother	circuit
income	southeast
ore	spoken
origin	throat
canoe	fifteen
pain	flour

Word Study   Homophones

ore = rocks with minerals   flour = ground grain
or = a conjunction "this or that" flower = bloom on a
oar = boat paddle   plant

Variant forms

relationships   beamed   beaming   beams
borrow borrower borrowers   explorer
grandmothers   incomes
ores   origins
canoeist canoes   pained pains
pastured pastures pasturing   penned penning pens
recordings   selections
circuits   southeastern
throats   floured

Review: Word Study in Lessons 116, 117, & 118.

Laguna Beach Educational Books 245 Grandview, Laguna Beach, California 92651

Instant Words 1906-1925

impossible	truth
peaks	youth
welcome	bacteria
brief	fierce
classroom	furniture
fog	invention
importance	reduced
independence	scouts
remainder	aloud
rocky	buried

Word Study   Phonogram "-out"

scout	shout	spout
about	pout	trout

Note: While the /ou/ sound is frequently spelled "ou", it can also be spelled "ow" as in "powder".

Variant forms

impossibly	peak peaked
welcomed welcomes welcoming	briefed briefing
classrooms	briefly briefs
fogging fogs	remainders
fiercely fierceness	inventions
fiercer fiercest	reduce reduces reducing
scout scouting	buries bury burying

Review: Check Personal Spelling Lists. Partners quiz.

Laguna Beach Educational Books 245 Grandview, Laguna Beach, California 92651

Instant Words 1926-1945

cousin	seek
declared	suffered
marbles	tend
Sunday	courage
hate	damage
lamp	magazine
patient	palace
pink	tape
rats	couple
scattered	fool

Word Study   Phonogram "-eek"

seek	week	Greek
peek	cheek	sleek

Note: The phonogram "-eak" makes the same /ēk/ sound and gives some homophones "peek-peak" and "week-weak".

Variant forms

cousins	lamps
pinkish	declare declares declaring
marble	Sundays
hated hates hating	patiently patients
rat ratted	scatter scattering scatters
seeked seekers seeking seeks	suffer sufferer suffering
tended tending tends	sufferings suffers
damaged damages damaging	magazines
palaces	taped tapes taping
coupled couples coupling	fooled foolers fooling

Review: Selected Instant Words in Lessons 118, 119, & 120.

Laguna Beach Educational Books 245 Grandview, Laguna Beach, California 92651

Instant Words 1946-1965

football	**military**
leather	**observations**
opera	**sandwiches**
screen	**snapped**
sweeping	**vapor**
comfortable	**agriculture**
compass	**announced**
dragon	**atomic**
empire	**somewhat**
false	**tap**

Word Study   Phonics: Broad "o" sound spelled "a" before "l"

false	**fall**	**always**
also	**although**	**talk**

Note: The letter "a" before the letter "l" often makes the broad /ô/ sound, but not always, for example, "alone".

Variant forms

footballs
screened screening screens
comfortable
compasses
empires
sandwich sandwiched
vapors
announce announces announcing

operas
sweep sweeper
sweepers sweeps
dragons
observation observational
snap snapping snaps
agricultural
tapped tapping taps

Review: Word Study in Lessons 119, 120, & 121.

Laguna Beach Educational Books 245 Grandview, Laguna Beach, California 92651

Instant Words 1966-1985

acres	issue
decision	thy
glow	alphabet
thirty	alphabetical
tin	attend
blew	brick
chosen	dimes
Columbus	happening
doll	joke
duty	juice

Word Study   Phonics: Blend "bl"

blew	blood	black
blow	block	blanket

Note: "Blew" is a homophone of "blue".

Variant forms

acre	decisions
glowed glowing glows	thirties
tinned tins	dolled dolls
duties	issued issues issuing
alphabetic alphabets	alphabetically
attended attending attends	bricks
dime	happenings
joked jokes joking	juices

Review: Check Personal Spelling Lists. Partners quiz.

Laguna Beach Educational Books 245 Grandview, Laguna Beach, California 92651

Instant Words 1986-2005

machinery	tonight
religion	bud
steep	carved
cheer	description
hospital	ghost
ought	leaf
saddle	location
settlement	seal
sewing	apartment
split	grand

Word Study Phonics: /j/ sound spelled "g"

religion	gym	large
general	age	gentleman

Note: The letter "g" often makes the /j/ sound before an "i", "e", or "y". But before an "a", "o", or "u", it usually makes the /g/ sound, as in "go", "gas", "gun".

Variant forms

religions	steeped steeper steepest
cheered cheering cheers	steeply steepness
hospitals	saddled saddles saddling
settlements	sew sewed
splits splitting	budding
carve carvers carves	descriptions
carving carvings	ghosts
locations	sealed sealer
apartments	sealing seals
grandly	

Review: Selected Instant Words in Lessons 121, 122, & 123.

Laguna Beach Educational Books 245 Grandview, Laguna Beach, California 92651

Instant Words 2006-2025

hollow	worn
voyage	calm
anyway	drifted
difficulty	labor
sink	museum
cliff	approximately
harmony	arithmetic
integers	billion
tense	coach
transportation	crash

Word Study Spelling Pattern Final "y"

"y" usually makes long /ē/ sound:

difficulty harmony approximately machinery

But final "ay" makes long /ā/ sound: **anyway say**

Note: Remember that a single "e" at the end of a word is usually silent. See the words in this Lesson: "voyage" and "tense".

Variant forms

hollowed hollowing
hollowness   hollows
difficulties
cliffs
integer
calmed calmer calmest
calming calmly calmness calms
labored laboring labors
approximate approximated
coached coaches coaching

voyaged voyager voyagers
voyages   voyaging
sinking sinks
harmonies
tensed tensely
tenses tensing
drift drifting drifts
museums
billions
crashed crashes crashing

Review: Word Study in Lessons 122, 123, & 124.

Laguna Beach Educational Books 245 Grandview, Laguna Beach, California 92651

Level 5

Lessons 126-160

This Section contains 35 Lessons
Each Lesson contains:
- **20 Spelling Words**
  Instant Words Ranks 2026-2725

- **Word Study**
  homophones, homographs, suffixes,
  multiple meanings, prefixes, spelling
  patterns, plurals, synonyms, word origins,
  contractions, word meanings, etc.

- **Review suggestions**

Instant Words 2026-2045

stove	complex
dashed	council
instant	film
organs	pause
scared	Christian
somewhere	cookies
assume	deposits
donkey	owl
shelter	recall
address	salmon

Word Study   Homophones (words that sound the same)

council = a group that rules or makes laws.

counsel = to advise someone; a lawyer.

Note: Watch out for the silent "l" in "salmon".

Variant forms

stoves
instantly
organ
assumed   assumes   assuming
sheltered   sheltering   shelters
complexes
councils
paused   pauses   pausing
cookie
owls
recalled   recalling   recalls

dash   dasher
dashes   dashing
scare   scares   scaring
donkeys
addressed   addresses
addressing
filmed   filming   films
Christians
deposit   deposited
depositing

Review: Start students keeping a Personal Spelling List. See Appendix 5 for suggestions.

Laguna Beach Educational Books 245 Grandview, Laguna Beach, California 92651

Instant Words 2046-2065

skirt	due
switch	errors
delivered	gallons
helpful	hero
percent	image
prefer	mental
pure	tough
rear	echo
vitamins	governor
aware	heaven

Word Study   Suffix "or" - "er"

The suffix sound /ər/ spelled "or" often means "one who does something". For example, one who governs is a "governor", one who acts is an "actor". The same suffix /ər/ is also sometimes spelled "er" as in "teacher" or "painter".

Variant forms

skirted   skirting   skirts
deliver   delivering   delivers
percents
purer   purest
reared   rearing
awareness
error
heroes
mentally
echoed   echoes   echoic   echoing
heavens

switched   switches
switching
preferred   preferring
prefers
vitamin
dues
gallon
images
tougher   toughest   toughness
governors

Review: Most of the major phonics rules are covered in Lessons 1-55. The chart in Appendix 7 gives a more complete phonics skills listing, which can serve as a phonics review.

Laguna Beach Educational Books 245 Grandview, Laguna Beach, California 92651

Instant Words 2066-2085

photograph	goose
relations	June
seam	ma
communication	mercury
Communist	neat
exchange	numerator
positive	religious
begun	rider
congruent	silk
culture	brass

Word Study   Homophones

seam = a mark or line where two things join.

seem = to appear to be: "He seems ok."

Note: Watch out for the /ng/ sound and spelling in "exchange" and the double "ss" in "brass".

Variant forms

photographs
seamed   seams
Communists
positives
cultured cultures culturist
numerators
riders
brasses

relation
communications
exchanged   exchanges
exchanging
neater neatest
neatly neatness
silks

Review: Another approach to teaching phonics is through phonograms. They are used heavily up through Lesson 125. A chart summarizing phonograms taught (an index) can be found in Appendix 7.

Laguna Beach Educational Books 245 Grandview, Laguna Beach, California 92651

Instant Words 2086-2105

chamber	interior
effective	opportunity
harvest	singer
mice	steer
rectangle	stomach
stairs	lightning
vibrate	nuts
afterwards	pleasure
creek	previous
entry	protein

Word Study   Homograph (words that are spelled the same, sound the same, but have a different origin and different meaning)

steer[1] = to guide or direct: "steer a car".

steer[2] = young male of beef cattle.

Note: Homographs have separate entries in a dictionary.

Variant forms

chambered chambers
harvested harvesting harvests
stair
afterward
creeks
interiors
singers
stomachs
nut
previously

effectively effectiveness
rectangles
vibrated vibrates
vibrating
entries
opportunities
steered steering steers
lightning
pleasures
proteins

Review: Selected Instant Words in Lessons 126, 127, & 128.

Laguna Beach Educational Books 245 Grandview, Laguna Beach, California 92651

Instant Words 2106-2125

addends	occasion
command	tissue
compute	anywhere
elected	assembly
freezing	blade
gulf	faint
hatch	occasionally
laboratory	republic
loss	ridge
nervous	slept

Word Study   Multiple meanings

blade = [1]cutting part of a knife, a sword
[2]a leaf of grass

faint = [1]dim or not clear
[2]to become unconscious

Note: Many word have multiple meanings. The difference between multiple meanings and homographs is that homographs have a different word origin and a separate dictionary entry. "Addends" are numbers added together.

Variant forms

addend
computed computes computing
freeze freezes
hatched hatches hatching
losses
occasions
assemblies
fainted fainter faintest
fainting faintly faints
ridges

commanding commands
elect electing elects
gulfs
laboratories
nervously nervousness
tissues
blades
occasional
republics

Review: Word Study in Lessons 126, 127, 128, & 129.

Laguna Beach Educational Books 245 Grandview, Laguna Beach, California 92651

Instant Words 2126-2145

speaker	bubbles
tons	dioxide
whip	essential
acid	noon
July	prairie
luck	purchase
universe	screamed
accompany	solar
astronauts	thermometer
bananas	upward

Word Study   Prefix "up"

"up" means "up" as in upward, upgrade, uphold, update, uphill, upkeep.

Word meanings:

"astronauts" = pilot or crew of a spacecraft.

"dioxide"   = chemical with two atoms of oxygen

Variant forms

speakers	ton
whipped whipping whips	acids
universes	accompanied accompanies
astronaut	accompanying
banana	bubble bubbled
essentially essentials	bubbling bubbly
prairies	purchased purchaser
scream screamer screaming	purchases purchasing
thermometers	upwards

Review: Check to make sure each student is keeping a Personal Spelling List. See Appendix 5 for suggestions on Personal Spelling Lists. Partners can quiz each other on Personal Spelling Lists.

Laguna Beach Educational Books 245 Grandview, Laguna Beach, California 92651

Instant Words 2146-2165

apparently	international
beaver	plastic
committee	stuff
cord	volcano
enable	dissolved
hydrogen	lowlands
Israel	soup
occupied	active
thunder	clap
hop	claws

Word Study   Double letters

Watch out for the double letters in these spelling words: a<u>pp</u>arently   co<u>mm</u>i<u>tt</u>ee   stu<u>ff</u>   o<u>cc</u>upied di<u>ss</u>olved   ho<u>pp</u>ing   cla<u>pp</u>ing

Double letters in the middle of a word usually indicate that the consonant sound is at both the end of one syllable and the beginning of the next syllable. Example: clap-ping.

Variant forms

apparent
committees
enabled   enables   enabling
thundered   thundering   thunders
internationally
stuffed   stuffing   stuffs
dissolve   dissolves   dissolving
soups
clapped   clapping   claps

beavers
cordless   cords
occupies   occupy   occupying
hopped   hopping   hops
plastics
volcanoes
lowland
actively
claws   clawed   clawing

Review: Selected Instant Words in Lessons 129, 130, & 131.

Laguna Beach Educational Books 245 Grandview, Laguna Beach, California 92651

Instant Words 2166-2185

fibers	**private**
reveal	**slice**
servant	**vibrations**
worms	**anybody**
content	**defeated**
county	**definite**
dawn	**kingdom**
gasoline	**prepositional**
generation	**ribbon**
plow	**struck**

Word Study   Multiple meanings

dawn - (noun)[1]   time when the sun comes up
      - (verb)[2]   to become aware; "it dawned on him"

plow - (noun)[1]   a farm implement for breaking soil
      - (verb)[2]   to use a plow

Note: Some words can be either a noun or a verb, depending on how they are used. The meaning can change with the use.

Variant forms

fiber	revealed revealing reveals
servants	worm
contents	counties
dawned dawning dawns	gasolines
generations	plowed plowing plows
privately	sliced slices slicing
vibration	defeat defeating defeats
definitely	kingdoms
preposition prepositions	ribbons

Review: Word Study in Lessons 130, 131, & 132.

Laguna Beach Educational Books 245 Grandview, Laguna Beach, California 92651

Instant Words 2186-2205

stuck	lucky
lumber	memory
mathematics	peaches
merchant	permitted
microscope	reaction
screw	shock
background	sketch
basis	admitted
distinguished	arrangement
fossils	conclusion

Word Study   Suffix adding - Double final letter

Examples: admit, admitted, admits, admitting.

The spelling rule is that you double the final letter before adding the suffix if:

1. The word has one syllable -like "admit".
2. The word ends in a single consonant -like "admit".
3. The word has a single vowel -like "admit".
4. The suffix begins with a vowel -
     "ed"   =   "admitted"
     "ing" =   "admitting"

Note: You don't double with a consonant when the word ends in a suffix "s" = "admits".

Variant forms

lumbered lumbering lumbers
microscopes
backgrounds
fossil
luckier
peach
reactions
sketched sketches sketching
admit admits admitting
conclusions

merchants
screwed screwing screws
distinguish distinguishable
distinguishes distinguishing
memories
permit permits permitting
shocked shocker
shocking shocks
arrangements

Review: Check Personal Spelling Lists. Partners quiz.

Laguna Beach Educational Books 245 Grandview, Laguna Beach, California 92651

Instant Words 2206-2225

maintain	plateau
mosquitoes	quantities
primitive	regarded
raw	royal
squirrel	staff
bundle	trial
cube	advantage
favor	distant
independent	enormous
loop	eventually

Word Study   Multiple meanings

blade $=$ [1] a pole or rod
                [2] a group assisting "a school staff"

raw $=$ [1] uncooked
                [2] damp weather
                [3] not trained

Note: The "eau" ending in "plateau" is from French and "eau" makes the long /ō/ sound as in "bureau" and "chateau".

Variant forms

maintained maintaining maintains   mosquito
primitives   squirrels
bundled bundles bundling   cubed cubes
favored favoring favors   independently
looped looping loops   independents
plateaus   quantity
regard regarding regards   staffed staffs
trials   advantages
distantly   enormously
eventual

Review: Selected Instant Words in Lessons 132, 133, & 134.

Laguna Beach Educational Books 245 Grandview, Laguna Beach, California 92651

Instant Words 2226-2245

Greece	published
legend	fed
nickel	germs
partner	northwest
challenge	performance
commas	preceding
dirt	tropical
explanation	cardboard
hotel	formula
plus	mad

Word Study   Plurals and "s" forms (third person singular of verbs)

For most plurals, just add "s". For example,
nickel-nickels, challenge-challenges, germ-germs.

But if the word ends in a "y" preceded by a consonant,
change the "y" to "i" and add "es". For example,
baby-babies, country-countries, carry-carries.

Variant forms

legends	nickels
partners	challenged challenger
comma	challenges challenging
explanations	hotels
publish publishes publishing	germ
northwestern	performances
precede preceded precedes	cardboards
formulas	madder maddest

Review: Word Study in Lessons 133, 134, & 135.

Laguna Beach Educational Books 245 Grandview, Laguna Beach, California 92651

Instant Words 2246-2265

male	goal
reed	weapons
understood	breeze
victory	bulb
zoo	cheeks
aside	companions
discussion	defined
dug	garment
economic	nurse
expert	pat

Word Study   Homophones

male = opposite of female   mail = letters
reed =   all grass   read = get meaning
from print

Phonogram "-eeze"

breeze   sneeze   squeeze
freeze   wheeze

Variant forms

males	reeds
victories	zoos
expertly experts	goals
weapon	breezed breezes
bulbs	cheek
companion	define defines defining
garments	nursed nurses nursing
pats patted patting	

Review: Check Personal Spelling Lists. Partners quiz.

Laguna Beach Educational Books 245 Grandview, Laguna Beach, California 92651

Instant Words 2266-2285

sandy	Soviet
skip	toad
stress	unknown
temple	worse
achieved	bet
bench	fans
jacket	Norway
magnetic	pale
quarts	palm
shark	seized

Word Study   Plurals and "s" forms adding "es"

For words that ends in "ch", "sh", "x", "s", or "z", add "es" (not "s").

bench-benches	stress-stresses
bush-bushes	box-boxes

Note: Spelling hint - adding "es" adds a syllable but just "s" doesn't.

Variant forms

skipped skipping skips	stressed stresses stressing
temples	achieve achieves
benches	achieving
jackets	quart
sharks	Soviets
toads	bets betters betting
fan fanned fanning	paled paler paling
palms	seize seizes seizing

Review: Selected Instant Words in Lessons 135, 136, & 137.

Laguna Beach Educational Books 245 Grandview, Laguna Beach, California 92651

Instant Words 2286-2305

somebody	frost
wolf	handsome
aim	hay
appropriate	league
beast	obviously
crust	paw
Mars	porch
thumb	treasure
beads	canyon
begged	dimensions

Word Study   Plurals and "s" forms for words ending in "f"

For words endings in "f", change the "f" to "v" and add "es".

wolf-wolves   leaf-leaves   thief-thieves

Variant forms

aimed aiming aims   wolves
appropriately   crusted crusts
thumbs   bead beaded
beg begging   frosted frosting frosts
handsomely handsomer handsomest   haying
leagues   obvious
pawed pawing paws   porches
treasured treasure   canyons
dimension dimensioning

Review: Word Study in Lessons 136, 137, & 138.

Laguna Beach Educational Books 245 Grandview, Laguna Beach, California 92651

Instant Words 2306-2325

rifle	stiff
swam	thrown
weren't	tire
behavior	astronomers
bore	conduct
colt	eagle
excellent	female
fork	Florida
liberty	ink
midnight	investigation

Word Study   Homographs

bore ^{1} = make a hole with a tool that keeps turning.
bore ^{2} = make someone weary by tiresome talk.

tire ^{1} = to use up strength or attention.
tire ^{2} = a band of rubber around a wheel.

Variant forms

rifles	behavioral
bored bores boring	colts
forked forkful forking forks	liberties
stiffly stiffness	tires
astronomer	conducted conducting
eagles	conducts
females	inked inking inks
investigations	

Review: Check Personal Spelling Lists. Partners quiz.

Laguna Beach Educational Books 245 Grandview, Laguna Beach, California 92651

Instant Words 2326-2345

minister	**medical**
portion	**neighborhood**
tobacco	**province**
tunnel	**September**
classified	**statue**
parade	**succeeded**
peninsula	**appeal**
repair	**attitude**
spite	**chose**
bang	**contest**

Word Study   Plurals with no change

A few words are exactly the same for singular and plural

tobacco	**deer**	**fish**
sheep	**Chinese**	**series**

Note: The final /o͞o/ sound in "statue" is spelled the same as the ending sound in "blue", "glue", and "true".

Variant forms

ministers	portions
tunneling tunnels	classifies classify
paraded parades parading	classifying
peninsulas	repaired repairing
banged banging bangs	repairs
neighborhoods	provinces
statues	succeed succeeding
appealed appealing appeals	succeeds
attitudes	contested contests

Review: Selected Instant Words in Lessons 138, 139, & 140.

Laguna Beach Educational Books 245 Grandview, Laguna Beach, California 92651

Instant Words 2346-2365

contraction	**typical**
drugs	**vocabulary**
hemisphere	**wherever**
holiday	**additional**
navy	**dull**
pearl	**grazing**
splash	**width**
tiger	**cast**
airport	**code**
tender	**comparison**

Word Study   Capitalize proper nouns

any drug store → Smith's Drug Store
any navy   → U.S. Navy
any airport   → J.F.K. Airport
any pearl   → <u>The Pearl</u> (book title)

Variant forms

contractions	drug drugged
hemispheres	holidays
pearls	splashed splashes
tigers	splashing
airports	tenderly tenderness
typically	tendering
vocabularies	dulled duller
graze grazed	dullness dully
widths	casts
coded codes	comparisons

Review: Word Study in Lessons 139, 140, & 141.

Laguna Beach Educational Books 245 Grandview, Laguna Beach, California 92651

Instant Words 2366-2385

diver	associated
forever	diamond
jaws	ill
knight	impression
lever	insisted
authority	intended
concert	purple
considerable	rainfall
notebook	slant
patch	uniform

Word Study   Homophones

knight	=	military rank in the middle ages.
night	=	dark time between sunset & sunrise.
rain	=	water drops from sky - "it's raining today".
reign	=	a king's ruling period - "Queen Elizabeth's reign".
rein	=	a strap to guide an animal - "hold the horse's rein".

Variant forms

divers	jaw
knights	levers
authorities	concerts
considerably	notebooks
patched patches	associate associates
diamonds	associating
ills	impressions
insist insisting insists	intend intending intends
purples purplish	slanted slanting slants
uniformed uniformly uniforms	

Review: Check Personal Spelling Lists. Partners quiz.

Laguna Beach Educational Books 245 Grandview, Laguna Beach, California 92651

Instant Words 2386-2405

altitude	punctuation
backward	strain
forty	trust
garage	accompaniment
harm	April
hello	butterflies
hey	collar
illustration	proportion
knot	swung
Ohio	synonyms

Word Study   Synonyms

altitude	=	height		hello	=	hi, hey
backward	=	reverse		trust	=	believe
harm	=	injure		strain	=	tension

Note: Typically synonyms are words that mean the same, or nearly the same, as another word for one meaning of that word.

Variant forms

altitudes	backwards
forties	garages
harmed harming harms	illustrations
knots knotted knotting	strained straining strains
trusted trusting trusts	accompaniments
butterfly	collars
proportioned proportions	synonym

Review: Selected Instant Words in Lessons 141, 142, & 143.

Laguna Beach Educational Books 245 Grandview, Laguna Beach, California 92651

Instant Words 2406-2425

unhappy	**Arab**
verse	**crown**
anxious	**dock**
carriage	**meadow**
cone	**northeast**
corresponding	**Rome**
organisms	**cycle**
silly	**encouraged**
southwest	**Mediterranean**
web	**poetry**

Word Study   Prefix "un-"

unhappy	**unknown**	**unusual**
unfriendly	**unlike**	**unreal**

Note: Prefixes are a morpheme or meaning unit placed before a root (another morpheme). Sometimes both morphemes are obvious and easy to understand, sometimes they add fun or interest to the meaning of the word and sometimes they are obscure or downright confusing.

Variant forms

unhappily unhappiness	verses
anxiously	carriages
cones	correspondingly
silliness	southwestern
webbed webbing webs	Arabs
crowned crowning crowns	docked docking docks
meadows	northeastern
cycles cycling	encourage encourages
	encouraging encouragingly

Review: Word Study in Lessons 142, 143, & 144.

Laguna Beach Educational Books 245 Grandview, Laguna Beach, California 92651

Instant Words 2426-2445

pray	defense
shed	mysterious
sphere	priest
substitute	protection
swept	remarkable
unlike	representatives
adjust	slavery
affairs	vacation
bother	bass
cabbage	bitter

Word Study   Phonogram "-ept"

swept	slept	wept
kept	swept	adept

Note: "Bass" is a heteronym. Pronounced /băs/, it is a fish; and pronounced /bās/, it is a man singer with low notes.

Variant forms

prayed praying prays	shedding sheds
spheres	substituted substitutes
adjusted adjuster adjusting adjusts	substituting substitution
affair	substitutions
bothered bothering bothers	cabbages
defenseless defenses	mysteriously
priests	protections
remarkably	representative
vacationers vacations	bitterly bitterness

Review: Check Personal Spelling Lists. Partners quiz.

Laguna Beach Educational Books 245 Grandview, Laguna Beach, California 92651

Instant Words 2446-2465

brilliant	**secure**
bucket	**smart**
employed	**spear**
replacement	**civil**
somehow	**comfort**
wealth	**contract**
aboard	**data**
alarm	**former**
Junior	**ladder**
lawn	**oak**

Word Study　　　Spelling Pattern "board"

aboard	**skateboard**	**shipboard**
blackboard	**surfboard**	**headboard**

Note: A "board" is typically a thin long piece of wood, but it is a common combining form or part of a compound word.

Variant forms

brilliantly
employ employing employs
alarmed alarming alarms
lawns
smarter smartest smarting smartly
speared spearing spears
contracted contracting contracts
ladders

bucketfuls buckets
replacements
Juniors
secured securely
secures securing
comforted comforting
comforts
oaks

Review: Selected Instant Words in Lessons 144, 145, & 146.

Laguna Beach Educational Books 245 Grandview, Laguna Beach, California 92651

Instant Words 2466-2485

peered	colonists
policeman	commercial
precise	fever
signature	January
simplify	October
soap	seldom
suggestions	Brazil
weeds	contributed
August	Hawaii
classmates	sidewalk

Word Study   Word origins

<u>January</u> is named after the Roman God Janus with 2 faces looking ahead & behind.

<u>October</u> comes from Latin "octo" or "eight". It was the 8th month in the old Roman calendar (now it is the 10th month).

<u>August</u> is named after Augustus Caesar, a Roman Emperor.

Variant forms

peer peering peers	precisely
signatures	simplified simplifying
soaped soaps	suggestion
weed weeded weeding	classmate
colonist	commercially commercials
fevered fevers	Brazilian
contribute contributes contributing	sidewalks

Review: Word Study in Lessons 145, 146, & 147.

Laguna Beach Educational Books 245 Grandview, Laguna Beach, California 92651

Instant Words 2486-2505

survive	variations
violin	absorbed
wax	ancestors
clever	cheerful
diet	fertile
ease	file
fault	fortune
imagination	guy
Mexican	healthy
Philadelphia	highlands

Word Study   Homographs

file[1] = a drawer or folder for keeping papers in order
file[2] = a tool with tiny ridges for smoothing

guy [1] = a rope or wire used to steady something
guy [2] = slang for a fellow

Note: Remember that homographs are different words that look the same and sound the same, but have a different origin and separate dictionary entry.

Variant forms

survived survives surviving
waxed waxes waxing
dieters diets
eased easing
imaginations
variation
ancestor
fertility
fortunes
highland

violins
cleverer cleverest
cleverly cleverness
faulted faulting faults
Philadelphian
absorb absorbing absorbs
cheerfully cheerfulness
filed files filing
guys
healthier healthiest
healthily

Review: Check Personal Spelling Lists. Partners quiz.

Laguna Beach Educational Books 245 Grandview, Laguna Beach, California 92651

Instant Words 2506-2525

mechanical	conquered
mystery	foolish
Pennsylvania	glue
soul	lightly
submarine	ounces
symphony	pace
we'd	picnic
adapted	policy
birth	cylinder
concept	eleven

Word Study　　Contractions

we'd	= we would	we've	= we have
he'd	= he would	they've	= they have
you'd	= you would	would've	= would have

Note: Contractions are used when writing down speech, particularly informal speech.

Variant forms

mechanical	mysteries
souls	submarines
symphonies	adapt adapting adapts
births	concepts
conquer conquering	foolishly foolishness
glued glues gluing	ounce
paced pacer paces pacing	picnickers picnicking
policies	picnics
cylinders	

Review: Selected Instant Words in Lessons 147, 148, & 149.

Laguna Beach Educational Books 245 Grandview, Laguna Beach, California **92651**

Instant Words 2526-2545

evil	mate
fashion	pride
nitrogen	shallow
parentheses	shelf
Venus	techniques
boundary	wake
conductor	amazing
costume	Britain
display	civilization
good-by	clause

Word Study   Spelling Pattern "good-by"

This word can be spelled either "good-by" or "good-bye". Both spellings use a hyphen, as do some other good words like: good-looking, good-sized, and good-for-nothing, but there is no hyphen in: good morning, Good Friday, good will, or make good.

Variant forms

evilly evils	fashioned fashioning
boundaries	fashions
conductors	costumes
displayed displaying displays	good-byes
mates mating	prided
shallower shallows	technique
waked waking	amaze amazed
civilizations	amazes amazingly
clauses	

Review: Word Study in Lessons 148, 149, & 150.

Laguna Beach Educational Books 245 Grandview, Laguna Beach, California 92651

Instant Words 2546-2565

crow	Senator
halfway	truly
heels	wiped
role	autumn
yarn	bunch
automatic	crocodile
brake	dirty
election	expedition
hut	fireplace
Missouri	kitten

Word Study   Homophone "heel"

heel = [1]back of foot; [2]lean to one side
heal = to cure or make healthy
he'll = contraction for "he will"

Note: Watch out for that silent "n" at the end of "autumn".

Variant forms

crowed   crowing   crows
roles
automatically
elections
Senators
bunched   bunches   bunching
crocodiles
expeditions
kittens

heel   heeled
yarns
braked   brakes   braking
huts
wipe   wiper   wipers
wipes   wiping
dirtier   dirtiest
fireplaces

Review: Check Personal Spelling Lists. Partners quiz.

Laguna Beach Educational Books 245 Grandview, Laguna Beach, California 92651

Instant Words 2566-2585

lamb	Arctic
perimeter	attractive
pirates	behave
professor	belief
swamp	buck
torn	cart
twins	coil
colonel	dairy
lad	hawk
weary	horizontal

Word Study   Unphonetic words

colonel is pronounced /kur´nel/ even though there is no "r" in it and the middle "o" is worthless.

lamb has a silent "b" at the end.

belief /bi lēf´/ - it is unusual for the first single "e" to make the short /i/ sound or the "ie" to make the long /ē/ sound.

Variant forms

lambs   perimeters
pirate   pirating   professors
swamped   swamping   swamps   twin
lads   wearied   wearies
attractively   attractiveness   wearily   weariness
behaved   behaves   behaving   beliefs
bucked   bucking   bucked   bucking
carted   carter   coiled   coiling   coils
dairies   hawks
horizontally

Review: Selected Instant Words in Lessons 150, 151, & 152.

Laguna Beach Educational Books 245 Grandview, Laguna Beach, California 92651

Instant Words 2586-2605

Illinois	pitcher
rail	rage
reference	rank
suitable	ribs
thrust	sack
bumps	treaty
clerk	tremendous
gay	wilderness
instructions	channel
mayor	chocolate

Word Study Homographs

pitcher = container for pouring liquid
pitcher = throws a baseball

rank = foul smelling, course manner
rank = indicates

rail = handrail or metal track
rail = complain bitterly

Note: Watch out for the "s" at the end of "Illinois" - it is silent.

Variant forms

railed rails
thrusting thrusts
clerks
instruction instructional
raged rages raging
rib ribbed ribbing
treaties
channeled channels

references
bump bumping
gayer gayest
pitchers
ranked ranking ranks
sacked sacking sacks
tremendously

Review: Word Study in Lessons 151, 152, 153.

Laguna Beach Educational Books 245 Grandview, Laguna Beach, California 92651

Instant Words 2606-2625

complicated	witch
festival	benefit
frequency	fairy
frontier	feast
intervals	Friday
merry	latitude
pigeons	lizards
possession	ourselves
radiation	skeleton
steal	trumpet

Word Study   Homophones

merry = happy   marry = join together
Mary = girl's name

steal = take unlawfully   steel = strong metal

Note: "Witch" and "which" often sound the same, but sometimes they are pronounced /wich/ and /hwich/.

Variant forms

festivals   frequencies
frontiers   interval
merrily   pigeon
possessions   radiations
stealer   stealing   steals   witches
benefitted   benefits   fairies
feasted   feasting   feasts   Fridays
latitudes   lizard
skeletons   trumpeted   trumpeter
                                 trumpeters   trumpeting
                                 trumpets

Review: Check Personal Spelling Lists. Partners quiz.

Laguna Beach Educational Books 245 Grandview, Laguna Beach, California 92651

Instant Words 2626-2645

curled	bedroom
curtain	Bible
musicians	mom
obey	site
professional	trim
reward	uranium
rid	warriors
senate	batter
unique	berries
barrel	dramatic

Word Study   Antonyms

curled - straight   mom - dad
obey - disobey   batter - pitcher
unique - common   warriors - peace
                                            makers

Note: This "site" means place or location and "sight" is the act of seeing.

Variant forms

curl curls   curtained curtains
musician   obeyed obeying obeys
professionally professionals   rewarded rewarding
ridding   rewards
uniquely uniqueness   barrels
bedrooms   Bibles
sites   trimmed trimmer
warrior   trimmers trimming
battered battering batters   trimmings trims
berry   dramatically

Review: Selected Instant Words in Lessons 153, 154, & 155.

Laguna Beach Educational Books 245 Grandview, Laguna Beach, California 92651

Instant Words 2646-2665

fisherman	**bold**
glaciers	**camel**
lively	**cargo**
oven	**justice**
permanent	**moth**
polished	**pad**
stable	**rang**
traders	**tag**
ugly	**treatment**
awake	**urged**

Word Study   Morpheme (meaning unit) - "-men", "-er" mean "one who"

"-men" : **fishermen**   **"-er"** : **trader**
       : **boatmen**   : **polisher**
       : **plowmen**   : **singer**

Note: "-er" also has a comparative meaning. For example, big-bigger, fast-faster.

Variant forms

glacier   livelier liveliest
ovens   liveliness
permanently   polish polishes polishing
stables   trader
awakes   awaking   bolder boldest boldly
camels   boldness
cargoes   cargos   justices
moths   padded padding pads
tagged tagging tags   treatments
urge urges urging

Review: Word Study in Lessons 154, 155, & 156.

Laguna Beach Educational Books 245 Grandview, Laguna Beach, California 92651

Instant Words 2666-2685

advice	zone
aluminum	computer
Denmark	conflict
faith	delicate
homonyms	fleet
rare	gentleman
responsible	insert
sunshine	lap
they'd	moisture
westward	November

Word Study Word meanings

gentleman = one of good family, a term of politeness or respect

homonym = older term now superseded by "homophone", could include "homograph"

November = from Latin "novem" meaning nine, originally the 9th month in the old Roman calendar (now the 11th month).

Variant forms

faiths
rarer rarest
computers
delicately
inserted inserting inserts

homonym
zones zoning
conflicting conflicts
fleets
lapped lapping laps

Review: Check Personal Spelling Lists. Partners quiz.

Laguna Beach Educational Books 245 Grandview, Laguna Beach, California 92651

Instant Words 2686-2705

precious	sleeve
refrigerator	ax
cherry	contact
crayon	emperor
intersection	Eskimos
laughter	holy
moist	intersect
oxen	plot
platform	rename
responsibility	resistance

Word Study Prefix "re-" (means "again" or "back"); pronounced /ri/ or /rē/

rename = to name again
refrigerator = machine to cool again
responsibility = promise to return again
resistance = to stand again

Note: The prefix "inter-" means between. Hence, "intersect" means to cut or section between a whole, making it into parts.

Variant forms

refrigerators	cherries
crayons	intersections
ox	platforms
responsibilities	sleeves sleeveless
axes	contacted contacts
emperors	Eskimo
intersected intersecting intersects	plots plotted plotting
renamed renaming	

Review: Selected Instant Words in Lessons 156, 157, & 158.

Laguna Beach Educational Books 245 Grandview, Laguna Beach, California 92651

Instant Words 2706-2725

upset	ceiling
worship	convinced
battery	expensive
bull	hen
Netherlands	literature
peaceful	lump
pyramid	meanwhile
sword	paste
woke	rewrite
blossoms	secretary

Word Study   Origins

secretary -   same root as "secret"; originally an official who could keep secrets

Netherlands - "nether" means lower, the lowlands of Northern Europe

literature -   same root as "letter". Educated people know their letters and can read and write. They are literate.

Variant forms

upsets upsetting
batteries
bulls
peacefully
swords
ceilings
convince
hens
pasted pasting
secretarial secretaries

worshipped worshipper
worshippers worshipping
Netherlanders
pyramids
blossom blossomed
blossoming
expensively
lumped lumping lumps
rewriting

Review: Word Study in Lessons 157, 158, & 159.

Laguna Beach Educational Books 245 Grandview, Laguna Beach, California 92651

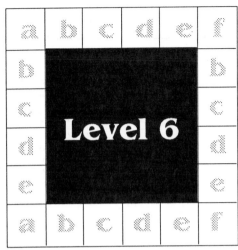

Level 6

Lessons 161-195

This Section contains 35 Lessons
Each Lesson contains:
- **20 Spelling Words**
  Instant Words Ranks 2726-3000 plus
  subject words, prefix words, & homophones

- **Word Study**
  homophones, word origins & prefixes

- **Review suggestions**

Instant Words 2726-2730

someday

basketball

damp

doorway

lane

Prefixes

<u>auto</u>**graph**

<u>auto</u>**mobile**

<u>auto</u>**matic**

<u>auto</u>**biography**

<u>auto</u>**crat**

States

Alabama, AL

Arizona, AZ

Arkansas, AR

Connecticut, CT

Delaware, DE

State Capitals

Montgomery

Phoenix

Little Rock

Hartford

Dover

Word Study   Prefix "auto" - means "self"

<u>auto</u>**graph** - a signature; "graph" means "write", it is "self-written".

<u>auto</u>**mobile** - a car; "mobile" means "move", it is "self-moving".

<u>auto</u>**matic** - operates by itself, or "self-operating" (mating).

<u>auto</u>**biography** - a biography or life story written by the subject himself or herself.

<u>auto</u>**crat** - a dictator or person who rules without consulting others or "self-rule".

Variant forms of Instant Words

basketballs	damper, dampness, dampens
doorways	lanes

Note: Have students learn to spell postal abbreviations for states along with full spelling of state name. Remember, postal abbreviations are two capital letters and no period.

Review: Start students keeping a Personal Spelling List. See Appendix 5 for suggestions.

Laguna Beach Educational Books 245 Grandview, Laguna Beach, California 92651

Instant Words 2731-2735

Massachusetts (MA)
threatened
wine
calf
commission

Homophones

ware
wear
where

side
sighed

States

Georgia, GA
Idaho, ID
Indiana, IN
Iowa, IA
Kansas, KS

State Capitals

Atlanta
Boise
Indianapolis
Des Moines
Topeka

Word Study   Homophones (words that sound the same)

ware (noun) - pottery or ceramic pieces; "dinnerware"
wear (verb) - to have on; "What shall I wear?"
where (adverb) - what place?; "Where is he?"

side (noun) (also adjective or verb) - a surface forming the
    outside; "the side of a house".
sighed (verb) - breath sound for sorrow or relief; "He sighed when
    he saw her."

Variant forms of Instant Words

| threaten threatening | wines |
| threateningly threatens | commissioned commissions |

Note: Since homophones sound the same but are spelled differently, it is important to give them in the context of a sentence. The word "where" can be pronounced with either a /w/ or /hw/ beginning sound.

Review: Most of the major phonics rules are covered in Lessons 1-55. A chart in Appendix 8 gives a more complete phonics skills listing which can serve as a phonics review.

Laguna Beach Educational Books 245 Grandview, Laguna Beach, California 92651

Instant Words 2736-2740

counter

fortunately

mathematical

otherwise

peanuts

Sign Words

cafeteria

entrance

explosives

storeroom

bike route

States

Kentucky, KY

Louisiana, LA

Maine, ME

Maryland, MD

Minnesota, MN

State Capitals

Frankfort

Baton Rouge

Augusta

Annapolis

St. Paul

Word Study   Compound words

Note that "storeroom" is a compound word, which means that there is no space between the two parts, while "bike route" is two separate words. It is part of spelling to know which are compound words and which are two words. A rough rule of thumb is that with frequent or common use, words become compounded.

Variant forms of Instant Words

countered counters   fortunate
mathematically   peanut

Note: Watch out for confusing abbreviations. The "M's" are particularly bad ("ME", "MD", "MN", plus Massachusetts is "MA" and Michigan is "MI").

Review: A number of state names are included in the Instant Words previously taught, but not with their abbreviations or capitals. Here are a few for review:

Alaska (AK)   Juneau
California (CA)   Sacramento
Colorado (CO)   Denver

Laguna Beach Educational Books 245 Grandview, Laguna Beach, California 92651

Instant Words 2741-2745

she'd	**Prefixes**
sleepy	<u>anti</u>war
version	<u>anti</u>social
anchor	<u>anti</u>slavery
annual	<u>anti</u>biotic
	<u>anti</u>freeze

States

Montana, MT
Nebraska, NE
Nevada, NV
New Hampshire, NH
New Jersey, NJ

State Capitals

Helena
Lincoln
Carson City
Concord
Trenton

Word Study   Prefix "anti-" - means "against" or "opposite"

<u>anti</u>war - against war
<u>anti</u>social - not social
<u>anti</u>slavery - against slavery
<u>anti</u>biotic - a medicine used against certain infections
<u>anti</u>freeze - a solution put in water to keep it from freezing

---

Variant forms of Instant Words

sleepier sleepily sleepiness   versions
anchored anchoring anchors   annually annuals

Review: With this Lesson, we will begin suggesting an every third week review pattern. You should select words in the previous three Lessons for review. The words might be words that presented extra difficulty or the review parts might be something easier like just the state abbreviations. Begin your review with Selected Instant Words from Lessons 161, 162, & 163.

Laguna Beach Educational Books 245 Grandview, Laguna Beach, California 92651

Instant Words 2746-2750

career

Irish

mild

possibly

primary

Homophones

profit

prophet

road

rode

rowed

States

New Mexico, NM

New York, NY

North Carolina, NC

North Dakota, ND

Oklahoma, OK

State Capitals

Santa Fe

Albany

Raleigh

Bismarck

Oklahoma City

Word Study   Homophones

profit - the money left after expenses are paid

prophet - a person who predicts the future

road - a long, smoothed surface made for traveling

rode - past tense for the verb "ride" (irregular past tense)

rowed - past tense for the verb "row" (regular past tense)

Variant forms of Instant Words

careers   milder   mildly
primaries

Review: A brief phonics review of the homophone words reminds us that:
1. The /f/ sound can be made by "ph", as in prophet.
2. The schwa sound /ə/ can be made by either the letter "i" or "e" in an unaccented syllable, as in the final syllables of "profit" or "prophet" (a common spelling problem).
3. The long /ō/ sound can be made by:
   A. The "oa" digraph, as in "road"
   B. The Final "E" Rule, as in "rode"
   C. The "ow" digraph, as in "rowed"

Laguna Beach Educational Books 245 Grandview, Laguna Beach, California 92651

Instant Words 2751-2755

procedure

ratio

rescue

scrambled

container

Sign Words

fire escape

nurse

pedestrian crossing

railroad

caution

States

Rhode Island, RI

South Carolina, SC

South Dakota, SD

Tennessee, TN

Utah, UT

State Capitals

Providence

Columbia

Pierre

Nashville

Salt Lake City

Word Study

The "Rhode" in Rhode Island is another homophone for "road", "rode", and "rowed" in Lesson 165.
"Pierre" is also a common boy's name in France.
A lot of town names end in "ville", which is French for city.
State names Utah and Dakota come from American Indian words.

Variant forms of Instant Words

procedures

rescued   rescuer   rescuers

rescues   rescuing

ratios

scramble   scrambling

containers

Review: A number of state names are included in the Instant Words previously taught, but not with their abbreviations or capitals. Here are a few for review:

Florida (FL)

Hawaii (HI)

Illinois (IL)

Tallahassee

Honolulu

Springfield

Laguna Beach Educational Books 245 Grandview, Laguna Beach, California 92651

Instant Words 2756-2760

inner

lazy

monster

spoon

alcohol

Prefixes

<u>under</u>neath

<u>under</u>cover

<u>under</u>ground

<u>under</u>pass

<u>under</u>wear

States

Vermont, VT

West Virginia, WV

Wisconsin, WI

Wyoming, WY

District of Columbia, DC

State Capitals

Montpelier

Charleston

Madison

Cheyenne

Washington

Word Study

A number of cities like "Washington" and "Charleston" end in "ton", which means "town". Note the schwa sound /ə/ in "ton" is spelled "o".

The District of Columbia is not a state, but in addressing letters you have to treat it like one. The same is true for Puerto Rico (PR) and Virgin Islands (VI).

Variant forms of Instant Words

lazier lazily laziness
spooned spoons

monsters
alcoholic alcoholics alcohols

Review: Here are more states in earlier Instant Words:

Massachusetts (MA)	
Michigan (MI)	Boston
Mississippi (MS)	Lansing
Missouri (MO)	Jackson
Ohio (OH)	Jefferson City
	Columbus

Also, review Selected Instant Words in Lessons 164, 165, & 166

Laguna Beach Educational Books 245 Grandview, Laguna Beach, California 92651

Instant Words 2761-2765

argument

ashes

coastal

dim

mule

Prefixes

microphone

microscope

microfilm

microsecond

microwave

Large U.S. Cities

Akron, OH

Albuquerque, NM

Amarillo, TX

Anaheim, CA

Anchorage, AK

Signs

taxi

warning

gentlemen

danger

information

Word Study

The prefix "micro" means small, but sometimes it means enlarging something small, as in "microphone" (phone=sound), or "microscope" (scope=view). In "microsecond", it is not only a small amount of time, but, more specifically, a millionth of a second; likewise, a "microgram" is a millionth of a gram. "Microwave" means any very short electromagnetic wave (1,000 to 3,000 mh), but children might know "microwave" as a cooking appliance that uses these waves.

Variant forms of Instant Words

arguments

dimly   dimmed   dimmer   dimness

ash

Review: Here are the last of the states taught earlier:
Oregon (OR)   Salem
Pennsylvania (PA)   Harrisburg
Texas (TX)   Austin
Virginia (VA)   Richmond
Washington (WA)   Olympia

Laguna Beach Educational Books 245 Grandview, Laguna Beach, California 92651

Instant Words 2766-2770

restaurant

spark

variable

agent

association

Homophones

aisle

I'll

isle

ant

aunt

Large U.S. Cities

Arlington, TX

Aurora, CO

Baltimore, MD

Birmingham, AL

Buffalo, NY

Signs

toll

sales tax

elevator

breakfast

coupon

Word Study

Watch out for the silent letters in "aisle" (in theater) and "isle" (island).

"I'll" is a contraction for "I will".

"Ant" is a bug; "aunt" is a relative.

The spelling of some students is improved if they learn to temporarily mispronounce or exaggerate syllables of some words; examples: rest-AU-rant, BREAK-fast, vari-ABLE.

Variant forms of Instant Words

restaurants	sparked sparks
variables	agents
associations	

Review: It is a good idea to review state abbreviations. Particularly confusing are those beginning with "M": ME, MD, MA, MI, MN, MS, MO, MT. You might want to have a student make a set of flash cards with the state on one side and the abbreviation or capital on the other.

Laguna Beach Educational Books 245 Grandview, Laguna Beach, California 92651

Instant Words 2771-2775

champion

continuous

crushed

devil

spare

Prefixes

bipolar

bicycle

binocular

bicentennial

biweekly

Large U.S. Cities

Charlotte, NC

Chattanooga, TN

Chicago, IL

Cincinnati, OH

Cleveland, OH

Signs

blasting

discount

hospital

passengers

private

Word Study

The prefix "bi" means two. Thus, bipolar means having two poles, like the earth. Since "cycle" means round, a bicycle has two wheels - not a unicycle or tricycle. "Ocular" means eyes, thus, most animals are binocular and binoculars magnify for both eyes. Bicentennial means every two centuries or 200 years, but be careful with "biweekly"; it is confusing because it can mean either every two weeks or twice a week!

Variant forms of Instant Words

championed   champions
crush   crushes   crushing
spared   spares

continuously
devils

Review: Selected Instant Words in Lessons 167, 168, & 169. You might also review prefixes taught thus far:

Prefix	Lesson	Prefix	Lesson
anti	164	un	145
auto	161	under	167
re	159	up	131

Laguna Beach Educational Books 245 Grandview, Laguna Beach, California 92651

Instant Words 2776-2780

thoroughly

anger

appointed

beef

cane

Large U.S. Cities

Colorado Springs, CO

Columbus, GA & OH

Dallas, TX

Dayton, OH

Homophones

sail (boat)

sale (price lower)

pause (time)

paws (animal feet)

lie (not true)

lye (chemical)

hair (on head)

hare (rabbit)

flea (insect)

flee (run away)

Word Study

These homophones illustrate many phonics principles:

Sound	Spelled	Example
Long "a" /ā/	"ai" or "ae"	sail; sale
Broad "o" /ō/	"au" or "aw"	pause; paws
Long "i" /ī/	"y" or "i"	lye; lie
Long "e" /ē/	"ea" or "ee"	flea; flee

Variant forms of Instant Words

thorough   thoroughness
appoint   appointing   appoints

angered   angering   angers
canes

Review: Pay some special attention to having each student keep up a Personal Spelling List. Pairs of students can quiz each other on words from Personal Spelling Lists.

Laguna Beach Educational Books 245 Grandview, Laguna Beach, California 92651

Instant Words 2781-2785

	Prefixes
core	**cent**ury
exception	**cent**
manager	**cent**imeter
morpheme	**cent**igrade
moss	**cent**ipede

Large U.S. Cities

	Signs
Des Moines, IA	**fire exit**
Detroit, MI	**emergency**
El Paso, TX	**smoking prohibited**
Fort Wayne, IN	**freeway**
Forth Worth, TX	**route**

Word Study

The prefix "cent" means hundred; the word "cent" means a coin that is one-hundredth of a dollar (also called a penny). Century is 100 years. Centimeter is 1/100 of a meter (.01 meter). Centigrade is a temperature scale with a hundred divisions between water freezing and water boiling that is used in Europe and everywhere the metric measurement system is used. Centipede is an insect that supposedly has 100 legs. The homophone of "cent" is "sent" (past tense of "send") and "scent" (meaning smell).

Variant forms of Instant Words

cores coring	exceptions
managers	morphemes
mosses	

Review: Variant forms of words that require an "s" to be added have three main rules:
1. For most nouns and verbs, just add "s"; for example, core/cores.
2. If the word ends in "ch", "sh", "x", "s", or "z", you must add "es"; for example, moss/mosses and box/boxes.
3. If the word ends in "y", preceded by a consonant, change the "y" to "i" and add "es"; for example, baby/babies.
See Spelling Rules in Appendix 1 for other exceptions.

Laguna Beach Educational Books 245 Grandview, Laguna Beach, California 92651

Instant Words 2786-2790

presence

rug

sixth

subset

sunny

Large U.S. Cities

Fremont, CA

Fresno, CA

Garland, TX

Grand Rapids, MI

Greensboro, NC

Homophones

beach (shore)
beech (tree)

trust (confidence)
trussed (tied up)

die (death)
dye (color)

creak (noise)
creek (stream)

chilly (cold)
chili (pepper)

Word Study   Synonyms

Synonyms are words that mean the same or nearly the same for one meaning of another word. Not all words have synonyms, but when they do, it is helpful to know them because they add to variety in writing and comprehension in reading. A few synonyms for some of our words are: rug=carpet, sunny=sunlit, trust=confidence, creek=stream.

Variant forms of Instant Words

rugs   sixths
subsets

Review: Phonics - the long /ē/ sound is made by:
1. "ea" as in beach, creak
2. "ee" as in beech, creek
The letter "y" makes the:
1. Long /ī/ sound in the middle of a word as in dye, cycle.
2. Long /ē/ sound at the end of a word as in chilly or sunny.
The suffix "-ed" sometimes makes the /t/ sound.

Review Selected Instant Words in Lessons 170, 171, and 172.

Laguna Beach Educational Books 245 Grandview, Laguna Beach, California 92651

Instant Words 2791-2795

bike

cub

furnace

invisible

nuclear

Prefixes

<u>inter</u>national

<u>inter</u>marriage

<u>inter</u>cultural

<u>inter</u>continental

<u>inter</u>nal

<u>inter</u>nist

<u>inter</u>n

<u>inter</u>ior

<u>inter</u>mission

<u>inter</u>cede

Large U.S. Cities

Hialeah, FL

Huntington Beach, CA

Jacksonville, FL

Jersey City, NJ

Kansas City, KS & MO

Word Study

The prefix "inter" means between, as in "<u>inter</u>national". "<u>Inter</u>nal" means within (between the sides), like "<u>inter</u>ior". An "<u>inter</u>nist" is a doctor specializing in illness within the body. An "<u>inter</u>n" is a trainee; someone between studying and practicing. "<u>Inter</u>mission" is the time between acts (literally, between sendings). "<u>Inter</u>cede" is to plead for someone (literally, a go-between).

Variant forms of Instant Words

bikes
furnaces

cubs
invisibility   invisibly

Review: Earlier, we saw that "-ton" at the end of a town name literally meant town; example, Huntington is "hunting town" and "-ville" meant city; example, Jacksonville is "jackson city". We see that some cities also just have the word "city" added to them like Kansas City. This is used particularly to distinguish the city from the state of the same name. Incidentally, "boro" at the end of some cities like Greensboro means borough, or small town.

Laguna Beach Educational Books 245 Grandview, Laguna Beach, California 92651

Instant Words 2796-2800

pilgrims

quotation

rainy

blast

cash

Homophones

doe

dough

do

surf

serf

Large U.S. Cities

Knoxville, TN

Las Vegas, NV

Lexington, KY

Long Beach, CA

Los Angeles, CA

Signs

reservations

detour

telephone

entrance

no thoroughfare

Word Study

A "doe" is a female deer, but "dough" is bread before it is baked (note this has the silent blend "gh"). "Do" is a musical note; "do" rhymes with "go" and "so" (long /ō/). A more common word is the heteronym "do" as in "I do". "Surf" is what the ocean has and a "serf" is a worker in feudal times. Remember that "er", "ur", and "ir" usually all make the same sound.

Variant forms of Instant Words

pilgrim
rainiest
cashed   cashes

quotations
blasted   blasting   blasts

Review: The suffix "-tion" is very common. The "ti" part of "tion" unfortunately isn't phonetically regular; it makes the /sh/ sound. Grammatically, "-tion" usually signals that this is a noun form of the word. For example, "The quotation was good". If you can put "the" or "a" in front of the word, it is a noun. The verb form of the word doesn't have "-tion"; for example, "I can quote him".

Laguna Beach Educational Books 245 Grandview, Laguna Beach, California 92651

Instant Words 2801-2805

chin

colonial

fancy

lens

shiny

Large U.S. Cities

Louisville, KY

Lubbock, TX

Madison, WI

Memphis, TN

Mesa, AZ

Prefixes

<u>tri</u>**ple**

<u>tri</u>**plet**

<u>tri</u>**angle**

<u>tri</u>**cycle**

<u>tri</u>**maran**

<u>tri</u>**logy**

<u>tri</u>**plex**

<u>tri</u>**plicate**

<u>tri</u>**pod**

<u>tri</u>**sect**

Word Study

The prefix "<u>tri</u>-" means three. "<u>Tri</u>plet is one of 3 children born at the same time. A "<u>tri</u>cycle" has 3 wheels; a "<u>tri</u>maran: is a boat with 3 hulls. A "<u>tri</u>logy" is a set of 3 plays, stories or novels ("logy"=word). "<u>Tri</u>sect" is to cut something into 3 parts ("sect"=cut).

Variant forms of Instant Words

chins
shine

fancied   fancier
fancies   fanciest

Review: Selected Instant Words in Lessons 173, 174, & 175.

All the cities which have been in Lessons 161 to present will help students a lot with map reading. A fun game is to have a group or class race to see who can locate a city on a map first.

Laguna Beach Educational Books 245 Grandview, Laguna Beach, California 92651

Instant Words 2806-2810

stanza

survey

tenth

auxiliary

clearing

Large U.S. Cities

Miami, FL

Milwaukee, WI

Minneapolis, MN

Mobile, AL

Montgomery, AL

Homophones

bark (tree)

barque (old boat)

choral (singing)

coral (reef)

load (heavy)

lode (ore vein)

pray (church)

prey (animal for food)

role (part in play)

roll (bread, list)

Word Study

A "barque" is a sailing ship, usually ancient. The letters "-que" making the /k/ sound is a French spelling. The British spell "check" as "cheque". The letter "c" regularly makes the /k/ sound, particularly before "a", "o", or "u", as in "coral" (reef), but "ch" also makes the /k/ sound in "choral" (singing), or "chemistry". Usually "ch" makes its own sound, as in "chief" or "chicken".

Variant forms of Instant Words

stanzas
tenths
clearings   clear

surveyed   surveying   surveys
auxiliaries

Review: Check to see if students are keeping a Personal Spelling List up to date. See Appendix 5 for suggestions.

Laguna Beach Educational Books 245 Grandview, Laguna Beach, California 92651

Instant Words 2811-2815

communicate

dining

divisible

flute

majority

Prefixes

semiannual

semicircle

semicolon

semiconscious

semiclassic

Large U.S. Cities

Nashville, TN

Newark, NJ

New Orleans, LA

Norfolk, VA

Oakland, CA

Signs

exit

self-service

pedestrians

hamburger

public

Word Study

The prefix "semi-" means half. So, a "semicolon" (;) is half a colon (:). "Semiannual" is half a year (or twice yearly) and a "semicircle" is half a circle.

Variant forms of Instant Words

communicated communicates
communicating
majorities

dine dined dines
fluted flutes

Review: Misspelling often occurs in the irregular or non-phonetic parts of words. Students can improve their spelling if they will use mnemonic, or memory devices like "The girl's name Ann is in semiannual"; "our class is only semiclassic"; "You have to be conscious that "SCIO" makes the /sh/ sound sometimes".

Laguna Beach Educational Books 245 Grandview, Laguna Beach, California 92651

Instant Words 2816-2820

overhead

radius

salad

soda

wreck

Large U.S. Cities

Omaha, NE

Philadelphia, PA

Phoenix, Az

Pittsburgh, PA

Portland, OR

Homophones

arc (curve)

ark (ship)

rap (hit)

wrap (cover)

real (original)

reel (spool)

reek (smell)

wreak (to inflict)

naval (navy)

navel (in belly)

Word Study

Mnemonics, or memory devices, can also be used in remembering homophone spelling. "Arc", which can be part of a circle, ends in a "c", which is part of a circle. A "reel" or spool is used in fishing to maybe catch an "eel". "Wrap" is bigger than "rap" because it has to go around something. "Al" is in the navy (naval).

Variant forms of Instant Words

salads   sodas

wrecked   wreckers   wrecking

Review: Selected Instant Words in Lessons 176, 177, & 178.
The final /k/ sound is usually spelled "ck", as in "wreck". But, as we see, the final /k/ sound can also be spelled "c", as in "arc" or "k", as in "ark".

Laguna Beach Educational Books 245 Grandview, Laguna Beach, California 92651

Instant Words 2821-2825

adopted

Austria

December

efficient

grave

Prefixes

monorail

monosyllable

monocular

monarch

monogamy

Large U.S. Cities

Raleigh, NC

Richmond, VA

Riverside, CA

Rochester, NY

St. Louis, MO

Signs

dentist

seafood

fragile

resume speed

clearance

Word Study

The prefix "mono-" means one or alone. A "monorail" has only one rail and a "monosyllable" is a word with one syllable. A "monarch" is a king or someone who rules alone. "Monogamy" means one marriage or having only one wife (not polygamy). A "monocular" is half a binocular; it's for one eye only.

Variant forms of Instant Words

adopt   adopting
efficiently

Austrian   Austrians
gravely   graves

Review: Exaggerating the pronunciation of syllables is another way of helping students remember how to spell a word. For other spelling aids, see General Comments About Teaching Spelling in the Introduction.

Note: In spelling city names, "Saint" is usually abbreviated "St."

Laguna Beach Educational Books 245 Grandview, Laguna Beach, California 92651

Instant Words 2826-2830

noisy

odor

prey

raft

shepherd

Large U.S. Cities

St. Petersburg, FL

San Antonio, TX

San Diego, CA

San Francisco, CA

San Jose, CA

Homophones

capital (money)

capitol (building)

cellar (basement)

seller (sells)

close (shut)

clothes (wearing)

vise (clamp)

vice (assistant)

tea (drink)

tee (golf)

Word Study

One way to help keep homophones straight is by commonness. "Capital" is the most common because it refers to the seat of government and money invested, while "capitol" is only a building in Washington. "Vice" refers to crime or an assistant like Vice President, but a "vise" is a fixed clamp. "Tea" is a popular drink, but a "tee" is something golfers use. We all wear "clothes", but sometimes we "close" a door.

Variant forms of Instant Words

noisier   noisiest   noisily   odors
preyed   preying   preys   rafts
shepherds

Review: Note a lot of world cities are named for saints. If the name is in English, it usually is abbreviated to "St.", but if the name is in Spanish, saint is spelled "San" for a male saint or "Santa" for a female saint.

Laguna Beach Educational Books 245 Grandview, Laguna Beach, California 92651

Instant Words 2831-2835

sweat

Swiss

Switzerland

ah

campaign

Large U.S. Cities

Santa Ana, CA

Seattle, WA

Shreveport, LA

Spokane, WA

Stockton, CA

Prefixes

prefix

preamble

prejudice

precaution

precollege

predawn

preconstruction

preexisting

preform

preassemble

Word Study

The prefix "**pre-**" means "before". So, a "**prefix**" is something fixed before the root of the word. A **preamble** is the written part before the main body of a document. **Prejudice** is judging someone or something before you know all the facts. The rest of the "pre-" words are pretty self-evident.

Variant forms of Instant Words

sweated   sweating

campaigned   campaigner
campaigning   campaigns

Review: Remember that prefixes usually don't change the spelling at all, they just add on. See Spelling Rules in Appendix 1. That's why there are two "e's" in "preexisting".
Review Selected Instant Words in Lessons 179, 180, & 181.

Laguna Beach Educational Books 245 Grandview, Laguna Beach, California 92651

Instant Words 2836-2840

entrance

helicopter

honey

numerous

nutrients

Homophones

vain (conceited)

vane (weather)

vein (blood)

soar (fly)

sore (hurt)

Large U.S. Cities

Tacoma, WA

Tampa, FL

Toledo, OH

Tucson, AZ

Tulsa, OK

Signs

tow-away zone

keep refrigerated

reduce speed

no admittance

parkway

Word Study

The 3 homophones, "vain", "vane", and "vein", are difficult because they are similar and abstract. "Vain" means conceited; perhaps you can visualize an "i" in it - a big "I". "Vein" also contains an "i", but since it refers to blood vessels, it is only a small "i". No "i"'s for a weather "vane". Having a "sore" is common and close, but to "soar" like a bird is less common.

Variant forms of Instant Words

entrances   helicopters
nutrient

Review: Notice that the letter "e" at the end of all 3 of the words, "entrance", "vane", and "sore", is silent. Silent letters cause a lot of trouble for spellers.

Laguna Beach Educational Books 245 Grandview, Laguna Beach, California 92651

Instant Words 2841-2845

perpendicular

proofread

they'll

underground

credit

Large U.S. Cities

Virginia Beach, VA

Wichita, KS

Yonkers, NY

Orlando, FL

Winston, NC

Prefixes

subtitle

submarine

suburb

subtract

subcompact

Signs

southbound

admission

alternate route

hardware

help wanted

Word Study

The prefix "sub-" means under. A. "subtitle" is a second title under the main title. A "submarine" goes under the ocean (marine=ocean). A "suburb" is an outlying part of an urban area. When you "subtract" you pull out something (tract=pull, as in tractor). A "subcompact" auto is smaller than a compact auto.

Variant forms of Instant Words

proofreader   proofreaders   proofreading   credited   credits

Review: Be careful that compound words like "proofread", "underground", or "southbound" aren't spelled with any space between the words.

Laguna Beach Educational Books 245 Grandview, Laguna Beach, California 92651

Instant Words 2846-2850

February

pollen

puppy

shone

texture

Countries

New Zealand

Nigeria

United Kingdom

Kenya

Egypt

Mathematics Words

diagonal

division

kilogram

minus

parallel

Social Studies

executive

legislative

revolt

tolerance

trait

Word Study

The letter "g" makes the /j/ sound before "i", "e", or "y", as in Germany and legislature. The other sound of "g" is the /g/ sound that we see in "diagonal" and "kilogram". Watch out for the spelling of the middle of "February". The two "l's" in "parallel" are parallel. "Kilo-" means thousand; a thousand grams is about 2.2 pounds.

Variant forms of Instant Words

puppies   textured   textures

Review: The prefix "re-" means back or again (Lesson 159). Revolt is movement back or against something. The prefix "di-" means two. Hence, one meaning of <u>di</u>vision is to <u>di</u>vide something into two or more parts.

Review Selected Instant Words in Lessons 182, 183, & 184.

Laguna Beach Educational Books 245 Grandview, Laguna Beach, California 92651

Instant Words 2851-2860

wages

cape

chalk

electronic

engaged

harness

landscape

outdoors

scarcely

stall

Homophones

cheap (inexpensive)

cheep (bird sound)

side (next to front)

sighed (sound)

wade (in water)

weighed (heavy)

sew (repair cloth)

sow (plant)

flair (talent)

flare (signal)

Word Study

"Cheep" and "sigh" are both a type of word called "onomatopoeia", or words that imitate sounds - a bird cheeps and a tired person sighs. Try using some mnenomics on homophones: "weighed" is longer than "wade", so it is heavier; "sow" has an "o" in it that is round like a seed; "flair" ends in "air" like an airplane pilot who has talent (the other flare is a flaming signal).

Variant forms of Instant Words

wage   waging
capes
landscaped   landscapes   landscaping
stalled   stalls
engage   engages   engaging

harnessed   harnesses
harnessing
chalked   chalking
electronically

Review: The final /k/ sound is usually made by the letters "ck" as in "back". However, in this Lesson, we see two other ways of spelling the final /k/ sound:
1. Just the letter "k", as in "chalk" (the "l" is silent to signal that the "a" makes the broad /ô/ sound.
2. Using the letter "c", as in "electronic".

Laguna Beach Educational Books 245 Grandview, Laguna Beach, California 92651

Instant Words 2861-2870

	Sign Words
Sweden	**express**
thirteen	**yield**
dense	**stairway**
despite	**fuel**
disappointed	**credit**
encyclopedia	**destination**
everyday	**flammable**
lid	**littering**
moreover	**two-way**
poison	**wayside**

Word Study

Double letters cause a lot of trouble in spelling. One source of double letters is vowel digraphs (2 letters that make one phoneme). We see that the long /ē/ sound is made by "ee", as in "Sweden" and "thirteen" (the other long /ē/ digraph is "ea", as in "seat"). Another source of double letters is when a syllable ends in one sound and the next syllable begins with that sound. We see that in "flam-ma-ble", "lit-ter-ing", and "dis-ap-point-ed". The way to remember the double letters in the words is to practice saying them syllable by syllable. Finally, we have the "ss" at the end of "express". We often see this when the root (not a plural) ends in the /s/ sound. Note "miss", "cross", "dress", and "distress".

Variant forms of Instant Words

Swede Swedes	densely denser
disappoint disappointing	encyclopedias
lids	poisoned poisoning poisons

Review: Most compound words simply put two words together, like "everyday", "moreover", and "stairway", but some less familiar double word terms, like "two-way", use a hyphen between the words. Worse yet, it is sometimes optional, as in "one way", or "one-way"; either is permissible.

Laguna Beach Educational Books 245 Grandview, Laguna Beach, California 92651

Instant Words 2871-2880

violet

ballet

Chile

convenient

jazz

lining

possessive

praise

sufficient

theater

Prefixes

supernatural

supersonic

supervise

superhuman

supernova

Geography

hemisphere

inlet

fertile

horizon

antarctic

Word Study

The prefix "super-" means "above or "more than".
Supernatural is more than natural - like ghosts. **Supersonic**
is above sound, like high pitched sound above the normal
hearing range (above 20,000 c.p.s.) or a speed above the
speed of sound (about 740 m.p.h.). **Supervise** - overseeing,
or vision from above; management. **Superhuman** is beyond
normal human - like Superman. **Supernova** is a super new
star, a giant new star.

Variant forms of Instant Words

violets		ballets	
Chilean	Chileans	convenience	
linings		possessives	
praised	praises	praising	sufficiently
theaters			

Review: Selected Instant Words from Lessons 185, 186, & 187.
          Watch out for silent letters. The final "t" in "ballet" is silent because it is a French word,
and a lot of French words don't sound the final letter; for example, Chevrolet and France. An English
word like "violet" does sound the final "t". The final "e" in "Chile" is sounded because it is a Spanish
word, and in Spanish there are very few silent letters. However, in English, an "e" at the end of a
word is frequently silent; for example, "praise" and "possessive".

Laguna Beach Educational Books 245 Grandview, Laguna Beach, California 92651

Instant Words 2881-2895

armed

caterpillar

chorus

director

economy

guitar

olive

timber

ye

awful

cannon

eighth

nevertheless

stern

target

Social Studies

grid

pollution

humidity

metropolitan

peon

Word Study

The Old English word "ye" sometimes means "you", as in "How are ye?" But "ye" also sometimes means "the", as in "Ye Olde Tea Shoppe".

Watch out for the initial "ch" digraph. In the case of our word "chorus", it makes the consonant /k/ sound. More often, "ch" makes the /ch/ sound, as in "chair". But sometimes (often in words of French origin), "ch" makes the /sh/ sound, as in "chef".

Variant forms of Instant Words

caterpillars	chorused choruses
directors	economies
guitars	olives
timbers	awfulness
cannons	eighths
sternly	targets

Review: Remember that the digraph "aw" at the beginning of "awful" makes the broad /ô/ sound which is the same sound made by "au", as in "auto", or "o", as in "off".

Laguna Beach Educational Books 245 Grandview, Laguna Beach, California 92651

Instant Words 2896-2910

unable

upstairs

wedding

administration

altogether

bath

introduction

parrot

severe

apron

colorful

density

emotional

gear

inland

Homophones

cite (summons)

sight (vision)

site (place)

cursor (pointer)

curser (swear)

Word Study   Homophones

"Cite" means summons to court, as in a traffic citation, or a reference, like citing an authority. "Sight" means vision or something seen; "The fire was a terrible sight." "Site" means a place; "This is a good site for a new house." "Cursor" is a pointer; "All computer screens have a cursor." "Curser" is someone who curses, hopefully not in school.

Variant forms of Instant Words

weddings
baths
parrots
aprons
densities
geared   gears

administrations
introduce   introductions
severely   severest
colorfully
emotionally

Review: Spelling rules about doubling the final letter before adding a suffix are hard to remember, but if you want an explanation of "wed - wedding", here it is.
        You double the final consonant if:
        1.   The word has one syllable.
        2.   The word ends in a single consonant (not "x").
        3.   The word has a single vowel letter.
        4.   The suffix begins with a vowel.

Laguna Beach Educational Books 245 Grandview, Laguna Beach, California 92651

Instant Words 2911-2925

apostrophe

blame

earthquake

elevator

relief

skunk

fist

ford

handwriting

modifiers

socks

afford

Apollo

brook

chromosomes

Signs

dangerous

intersection

pavement

cancel

receipt

Word Study

The old "i" before "e" rule doesn't always work, but it certainly applies to two words in this Lesson; "relief" and "receipt". If you recall the full rule, Put "i" before "e" except after "c".

Another phonics rule that often holds, is that the letter "c" makes the /k/ sound before "a", "o", and "u", and "c" makes the /s/ sound before "i", "e". and "y". Our spelling word "cancel" illustrates this nicely.

Variant forms of Instant Words

apostrophes	elevators
skunks	fists
fords	blamed blames blaming
modifier	sock socked
earthquakes	afforded affords
brooks	chromosome

Review: Selected Instant Words from Lessons 188, 189, & 190.
There are some common phonograms in this Lesson:

-ame	-ook	-ist	-ocks
blame	brook	fist	socks
came	look	mist	rocks
same	cook	twist	locks

Laguna Beach Educational Books 245 Grandview, Laguna Beach, California 92651

Instant Words 2926-2940

cruel	**overcome**
daylight	**sixty**
dying	**slid**
flavor	**underwater**
geometry	**veins**
helmet	**Prefixes**
horizon	**monorail**
kettle	**monarch**
moonlight	**monocular**
Oregon	**monologue**
	monosyllable

Word Study

The prefix "mono-" means "one".
Monorail has one rail (not two like a train).
Monarch is a single ruler, like a king.
Monocular is a glass (corrective lens) for one eye.
Monologue is a single person speaking.
Monosyllable is a word of only one syllable.

Variant forms of Instant Words

cruelest   cruelly   flavored   flavorful   flavors
geometries   helmets
horizons   kettles
overcomes   overcoming

Review: The "oo" digraph has two sounds:
  1. The "oo" in "moon" is the long /o͞o/ sound.
     (Some dictionaries use the symbol /ü/ for this sound.)
  2. The "oo" in "look" is the short /o͝o/ sound.
     (Some dictionaries use the symbol /u̇/ for this sound.)

Laguna Beach Educational Books 245 Grandview, Laguna Beach, California 92651

Instant Words 2941-2955

visible

worst

axis

cottage

forehead

Monday

queer

robot

solo

supreme

wolves

bacon

cabinet

chimney

continental

Science

algae

skeleton

pulse

preserve

focus

Word Study

Some words ending in the "f" sound form plurals by changing the "f" to "v" and adding "es".

wolf-wolves	self-selves
thief-thieves	life-lives

(but not words ending in "ff"; sheriff-sheriffs)

Did you know that Monday in olden times was "moon's day"? It is the day after the "sun's day".

Variant forms of Instant Words

visibly	queerest
robots	solos
supremely	cottages
cabinets	chimneys
foreheads	

Review: Poor little letter "x" doesn't have any sound of its own. Usually, it makes the consonant blend sound /ks/, as in "axis" or "box". Sometimes is makes a /gz/ sound, as in "example".

Laguna Beach Educational Books 245 Grandview, Laguna Beach, California 92651

Instant Words 2956-2970

derived	**Thanksgiving**
drank	**Christ**
kernel	**Colorado**
playground	**commerce**
sheriff	**nucleus**
sled	Geography
sprang	**vegetation**
duke	**urban**
glory	**suburb**
grasslands	**polar**
	neutral

Word Study

The usual way of forming the past tense is to put an "-ed" suffix at the end; for example, "play-played". However, many verbs change the form of the word (irregular). The past tense of "drink" is our word "drank". The past tense of "spring" is our word "sprang".

Variant forms of Instant Words

derive derives deriving   kernels
playgrounds   sheriffs
sledded   glories   glorying
grassland

Review: Proper nouns like "Thanksgiving", "Christ", and "Colorado" are always capitalized because they are very specific names of persons, places, or things. However, some words may or may not require a capital. Just any "sheriff" is not capitalized, but when it is used as part of a title, like "Sheriff Jones", it is. The same is true about just a "duke" or the "Duke of York".

Laguna Beach Educational Books 245 Grandview, Laguna Beach, California 92651

Instant Words 2971-2985

ripe

sixteen

Spaniards

technical

autoharp

crazy

downward

excuse

formal

inn

kite

medium

Michigan

speller

unexpected

Mathematics

kilometer

metric

circumference

divisor

grid

Word Study

Watch out for the schwa /ə/ plus /r/ endings. Note that the "er" ending of "speller" is indeed spelled "er", but at the end of some words, like "sailor", it is spelled "or". Note that the end of "formal" is spelled "al" to make the /l/ sound, while the same ending sound is spelled "le" in "cycle", "el" in "cruel", "ul" in "colorful", and "il" in "civil". Phonics knowledge is great, but it doesn't solve all problems.

Variant forms of Instant Words

Spaniard

craziest   crazily

formally

kites

spellers

technically

excused   excuses

inns

mediums

unexpectedly   unexpectedness

Review: Have an old fashioned spelling bee using words in this book to determine who is the champion speller.

Laguna Beach Educational Books 245 Grandview, Laguna Beach, California 92651

Appendix

This Section contains:

SPELLING RULES

Spelling rules are sometimes strange and wondrous and often more than a little complex. They mainly have to do with adding suffixes. Most of them are incorporated into elementary spelling lessons as incidental information, not necessarily to be memorized by the student. However, they can help the student to begin to see spelling patterns. The more important Rules have Capital Letters in front of them.

1. **PLURALS AND "S" FORM OF VERBS**
    A.   **Add "s" to most nouns and verbs. ex. cows, runs**
    B.   **Add "es" if the word ends in "ch", "sh", "x", "s", or "z". ex. box - boxes**
    For words ending in "y"
    C.   **If the word ends in a "y", preceded by a consonant, change the "y" to "i" and add "es". ex. baby - babies**
    d.   Note: Don't change "y" if a vowel precedes it. ex. key - keys
    e.   Also don't change "y" if it is in a proper noun. ex. one Kathy - two Kathys
    For words ending in "o"
    f.   For a few words ending in "o" add "es". ex. go - goes
    g.   However, for a lot of words ending in "o", just adding an "s" is OK because either spelling is correct. ex. banjos or banjoes
    h.   If the "o" is preceded by a vowel, just add "s". ex. radio - radios
    For words ending in "f"
    i.   For a few nouns ending in "f" (or "fe"), change the "f" to "v" and add "es". ex. leaf - leaves
    Other Plurals
    j.   Some foreign nouns have different plurals. ex. alumnus - alumni; index - indices
    k.   A few English nouns have different plurals. ex. foot - feet
    l.   A few nouns don't change for plurals. ex. deer - deer
    m.   Symbols form plurals with apostrophe ("'s") ex. 2's, ABC's

2. **POSSESSIVES**
    A.   **Add apostrophe "s" ("'s") to form possessive. ex. cow's**
    b.   If a plural word ends in "s", put the apostrophe after the "s". ex. One heroe's metal; two heros' metals

Laguna Beach Educational Books 245 Grandview, Laguna Beach, California 92651

3.   **ADDING SUFFIXES**

Basic Rule: Just add the suffix, except as follows:

Regular examples: want - wanted, wanting, wants

For words ending in "e"

A.   **Drop the final "e" if the suffix begins with a vowel. ex. rose - rosy; name - naming, named**

b.   Keep the final "e" if the suffix begins with a consonant. ex. safe - safely

c.   Keep the final "e" if a vowel precedes it. ex. see - seeing

d.   Drop the final "le" if the suffix is "ly" (no double "l"). ex. able - ably

For words ending in "y"

E.   **Change the "y" to "i" if "y" is preceded by a consonant. ex. carry - carried (Suffix here is "-ed")**

f.   Don't change the "y" to "i" if the "y" is preceded by a vowel. ex. joy - joyful

g.   Don't change the "y" to "i" if the suffix begins with an "i". ex. carry - carrying (Suffix here is "-ing")

For words ending in "c"

h.   Add a "k" before any suffix beginning with an "e", "i", or "y". ex. picnic - picnicking; panic - panicky

Doubling the final letter

I.   **Double the final consonant before adding the suffix if:**

      1.   the word has one syllable (or the final syllable is accented)

      2.   the word ends in a single consonant (not "x")

      3.   the word has a single vowel letter

      4.   the suffix begins with a vowel

Examples: brag - bragged; (not "x", box - boxing)

j.   You do not double the final consonant (Basic Rule applies) if:

      1.   the suffix begins with a consonant. ex. bag - bagful

      2.   the vowel has two letters. ex. rain - rained

      3.   the word has two final consonants. ex. hard - harder

      4.   the suffix begins with a consonant. ex. bag - bags

      5.   the final syllable is not accented. ex. benefit - benefited

k.   If the word has two syllables and is accented on the last syllable, treat it as a one syllable word. (See h. and j. above.) ex. admit - admittance

l.   If the word has two syllables and is accented on the first syllable, do not double the last letter (back to the Basic Rule). ex. equal - equaled

m.   The final "l" is kept when adding "ly". (This really restates the Basic Rule and Rule j., but it looks funny when you see two "l's".) ex. cool - coolly

Laguna Beach Educational Books 245 Grandview, Laguna Beach, California 92651

4.   **PREFIXES**
     Basic Rule: Prefixes never change the spelling, they just add on.
     a.   Even if it means having double letters. ex. misspell; illegible
     b.   Often the prefix "ex" and "self" use a hyphen. ex. ex-president;
             self-help

5.   **"EI" OR "IE" RULE (of dubious value)**
     Basic Rule: Write "i" before "e", except after "c".
             Example: chief; believe   Example of exception: receive
     a.   If the vowel sounds like long "a", spell it "ei". ex. neighbor; weigh
     b.   There are plenty of exceptions. ex. their; Neil; science; either; leisure

6.   **COMPOUND WORDS**
     Basic Rule: Keep the full spelling of both words. Don't use a hyphen.
             Example: ear + ring = earring; room + mate = roommate
     A more common usage or more specific meaning tends to put two words into a
     compound. ex. blackbird (one word); black car (two words)

Note: There is a whole other set of rules that concern spelling that are usually called
Phonics, which contain rules like the Final E Rule and consonant or vowel digraphs.
In addition to this, there is another set of rules for Syllable Division, which is related
to spelling. Besides this, there are a whole lot of Spelling Patterns which include
affixes and other morphological units, multiple phoneme units of words (like "tion")
and phonograms, and relatively rare single phoneme correspondences (phonics) like
"dge" making the /j/ sound in "fudge".

It is obvious from all the wonderful studies on "invented spelling" that
children and most beginning writers and readers do develop their own set of "rules".
For example, preschoolers often say "foots" showing that they have developed the
basic plural forming rule. These other sets of "Rules" might, just might, help
children and their teachers to show instances where more accurate and sophisticated
rules apply. The number of "exceptions" diminishes as more sophisticated rules are
developed, but don't panic; there will still be a large body of "exceptions", and we
should keep in mind that learning to spell is a lifelong process.

Laguna Beach Educational Books 245 Grandview, Laguna Beach, California 92651

GRAMMAR RULES

PLURALS OF NOUNS
1.   Add "s" to form plural. ex. cows
2.   For suffix exceptions, see Spelling Rule 1.
3.   A few English words have totally irregular or unique plurals.
    ex. child - children; tooth - teeth; man - men; deer - deer

PROPER NOUNS AND CAPITALIZATION
1.   The name of a person, place or thing is always capitalized.
    ex. Bill; Wednesday; Dr. Smith
2.   Don't change the spelling (ending) when adding suffixes.
    ex. "There are two <u>Marys</u> in our class.", or "Mr. <u>Fox's</u> Market."
    (You don't change "y" to "i" or add "es" to "x".)
3.   Capitalize the first word in a sentence.
4.   Capitalize all main words in a title. ex. "Peter Rabbit".

VERBS
1.   <u>Third person singular</u>, add "s". ex. "He walks."
    For exceptions to this "s" form of the verb, see Spelling Rule 1.
2.   <u>Past</u> add "ed". ex. "He walked."
3.   <u>Past participle</u> add "ed". ex. "He has walked."
4.   <u>Irregular verbs</u> don't follow above rules.

		Infinitive	Past	Past Participle
a.	some change all forms →	give	gave	given
b.	some never change →	hit	hit	hit
c.	some have the same, past and participle →	hold	held	held
d.	a few change past only →	run	ran	run

5.   <u>Present participle</u> adding "-ing"
    used after the verb "to be". ex. "He is walking."
6.   <u>Gerund</u> (noun form of a verb) also uses "-ing".
    ex. "He is walking hard."

ADJECTIVES
1.   When a verb is used as an adjective, add "-ing".
    ex. "The walking doll."

ADVERBS
1.   When an adjective (which modifies a noun) changes to an adverb
    (which modifies a verb), add "ly" to form the adverb.
    ex. (adverb) "He ran <u>quickly</u>."
    ex. (adjective) "The <u>quick</u> runner is here."

Note: Other grammar rules have to do with sentence formation (syntax) and punctuation. We have included only the above because they are related to spelling.

Laguna Beach Educational Books 245 Grandview, Laguna Beach, California 92651

PUNCTUATION MARKS

Period
1. At end of sentence. *ex. Birds fly.*
2. After some Abbreviations. *ex. Mr., U.S.A.*

Question Mark
1. At the end of question. *ex. Who is he?*
2. To express doubt. *ex. He weighs 250 (?) pounds.*

Apostrophe
1. To form possessive. *ex. Bill's bike*
2. Omitted letters. *ex. isn't*
3. Plurals of symbols. *ex. 1960's, two A's*

Parenthesis
1. Supplementary material. *ex. The map (see illustration) is good.*
2. Stronger than commas. *ex. Joe (the bad guy) is dead.*
3. Enclose numbers. *ex. Her car is (1) a Ford, (2) too slow.*

Colon
1. Introduce a series. *ex. He has three things: money, brains, charm.*
2. Separate subtitles. *ex. The Book: How To Read It.*
3. Set off a clause. *ex. He's not heavy: he's my brother.*
4. Business letter salutation. *ex. Dear Sir:*
5. Times and ratios. *ex. 7:45 A.M., Mix it 3:1.*

Semicolon
1. Stronger than a comma. *ex. Peace is difficult; war is hell.*
2. Separate clauses containing commas. *ex. He was tired; therefore, he quit.*

Quotation Marks
1. Direct quote. *ex. She said, "Hello".*
2. Titles. *ex. He read "Shane".*
3. Special words or slang. *ex. He is "nuts".*

Comma
1. Independent clauses. *ex. I like him, and he is tall.*
2. Dependent clause that precedes a main clause. *ex. After the game, we went home.*
3. Semi-parenthetical clause. *ex. Bill, the tall one, is here.*
4. Series. *ex. He likes candy, ice cream, and diamonds.*
5. Multiple adjectives. *ex. The big, bad, ugly wolf.*
6. In dialogue. *ex. She said, "Hello".*
7. Dates. *ex. July 4, 1776.*
8. Titles. *ex. Joe Smith, Ph.D.*
9. Informal letter salutation. *ex. Dear Mary,*
10. Letter closing. *ex. Yours truly,*
11. Inverted names. *ex. Smith, Joe*
12. Separate city and state. *ex. Los Angeles, California*

Exclamation Point
1. Show strong emotion. *ex. She is the best!*

Dash
1. Show duration. *ex. 1949-50, Rome-London*
2. Parenthetical material. *ex. The girl - the pretty one - is here.*
3. To show omissions. *ex. She called him a - - -.*

Laguna Beach Educational Books 245 Grandview, Laguna Beach, California 92651

SPEECH PRONUNCIATION

The Introduction suggests that pronouncing words properly can be a great help in spelling them correctly. This is true. Furthermore, you can sometimes exaggerate the pronunciation, even distort it a bit, to emphasize what letter should be used. A further help in pronunciation sometimes is to pronounce the word syllable-by-syllable. Here are a few other pronunciation suggestions:

1. Watch out for confusing words that have similar but not identical sounds; for example, celery & salary; finally & finely.

2. Don't add syllables that aren't there; for example, athlete (not athelete); laundry (not laundery).

3. Don't skip syllables that are there; for example, chocolate (not choclate); probably (not probly).

4. Don't skip letters that are there; for example, arctic (not artic); government (not goverment).

5. Don't reverse letters; for example, perform (not preform); tragedy (not tradegy).

6. Watch out for the schwa /ə/ or unaccented vowel sound. Because it causes a lot of errors in spelling lessons, it is often helpful to temporarily exaggerate the unaccented vowel letter (thereby making it not a schwa sound). Example: dollar; sponsor; benefit; definite.

7. For purposes of mnemonics or memory devices, it is sometimes helpful to even use a temporary incorrect pronunciation; for example, "Wednesday" might be pronounced "Wed-nes-day".

8. Take a little extra time with ESL students to see that they are pronouncing all the spelling words correctly.

Laguna Beach Educational Books 245 Grandview, Laguna Beach, California 92651

PERSONAL SPELLING LIST

Keeping a Personal Spelling List is a good idea for all students. It was suggested in the introductory material and it is mentioned in the Review sections of the Lessons.

The reasons for keeping a Personal Spelling List are that research has shown that most pupils' spelling errors consist of a relatively few trouble words. If these words are on the list, the pupil can learn them easier. If he or she has to look them up, it is much faster using a Personal Spelling List than a dictionary.

Also, a Personal Spelling List should contain words missed on the final spelling test. Thus, words which the pupil had trouble learning can be reviewed with the list or looked up easily.

The two main sources of words for a pupil's Personal Spelling List are:

1.   Words missed or requested when writing stories, and
2.   Words missed on the final tests.

If the pupil makes a booklet for keeping the Personal Spelling List with one page for each letter, it will be quickly observed that some letters like "s" use up a lot of space, and some letters like "q" or "z" use up very little space. Hence, some suggested page allotments are given in the following table for a large 60-page booklet or a small 18-page booklet.

Students can select spelling partners and partners can quiz each other from the student's own Personal Spelling List words. Words can be checked off if they are spelled correctly.

The Review section of the lesson suggests that the teacher check the Personal Spelling List of each student every 3 or 4 weeks to see that it is being updated (added to). This can be done while spelling partners are quizzing each other.

PAGES NEEDED FOR A 60-PAGE BOOKLET		PAGES NEEDED FOR AN 18-PAGE BOOKLET	
A	3	A	1
B	4	B	1
C	6	C	1
D	3	D	1
E	2	E	1
F	3	F	1
G	2	G	1
H	2	H	½
I	2	I	½
J	½	J	¼
K	½	K	¼
L	2	L	1
M	3	M	1
N	1	N	½
O	2	O	½
P	4 ½	P	1
Q	½	Q	¼
R	3	R	¾
S	8	S	2
T	3 ½	T	1
U	½	U	½
V	1	V	½
W	2	W	⅓
XYZ	1	XYZ	⅔

Laguna Beach Educational Books 245 Grandview, Laguna Beach, California 92651

PICTURE NOUNS

These words can be made into flash cards with the word on one side only or cards with the word on one side and the picture on the other. All these Picture Nouns occur in Lessons 1-20. They can be used for self-study or review: The student looks at the picture, spells the word, turns the card over to see if he was correct. Don't do too many at once. Also, these cards can be used for "thinking skills" or categorizing. Mix up several categories and have students sort out piles of cards that go together.

1. People
   boy
   girl
   man
   woman
   baby

2. Toys
   ball
   doll
   train
   game
   toy

3. Numbers
   one
   two
   three
   four
   five

4. Clothing
   shirt
   pants
   dress
   shoes
   hat

5. Pets
   cat
   dog
   rabbit
   bird
   fish

6. Furniture
   table
   chair
   sofa
   chest
   desk

7. Eating Objects
   cup
   plate
   bowl
   fork
   spoon

8. Transportation
   car
   truck
   bus
   plane
   boat

9. Food
   bread
   meat
   soup
   apple
   cereal

10. Drinks
    water
    milk
    juice
    soda
    malt

11. Numbers
    six
    seven
    eight
    nine
    ten

12. Fruit
    fruit
    orange
    grape
    pear
    banana

13. Plants
    bush
    flower
    grass
    plant
    tree

14. Sky Things
    sun
    moon
    star
    cloud
    rain

15. Earth Things
    lake
    rock
    dirt
    field
    hill

16. Farm Animals
    horse
    cow
    pig
    chicken
    duck

17. Workers
    farmer
    policeman
    cook
    doctor
    nurse

18. Entertainment
    television
    radio
    movie
    ballgame
    band

19. Writing Tools
    pen
    pencil
    crayon
    chalk
    computer

20. Reading Things
    book
    newspaper
    magazine
    sign
    letter

Laguna Beach Educational Books 245 Grandview, Laguna Beach, California 92651

PHONICS INDEX

VOWELS

Sound Phoneme	Lesson Number	Spelled Grapheme	Example
A Long /ā/	13	a-e	ate
A Long /ā/	47, 80, 81	ai	aid
A Long /ā/	16, 125	ay	way
A Short /ă/	1	a	add
A Broad /ä/	42	a (r)	arm
E Long /ē/	41	e	me
E Long /ē/	39, 107	ee	see
E Long /ē/	9, 32, 77	ea	eat
E Long /ē/	33, 45, 107, 125	y	carry
E Short /ĕ/	24	e	end
E Short /ĕ/	32, 77	ea	head
I Long /ī/	19	i-e	ice
I Long /ī/	45, 49	y	by
I Long /ī/	31	igh	height
I Long /ī/	110	i	find
I Short /i/	2, 110	i	ill
O Long /ō/	21, 87	o	old
O Long /ō/	58	o-e	code
O Long /ō/	79	oa	oak
O Long /ō/	10, 43, 87, 79	ow	own
O Short /o/	36	o	odd
O Broad /ô/	34	o	for
O Broad /ô/	118, 122	a	want
O Broad /ô/	118	au	auto
O Broad /ô/	29	aw	awful
OI Diphthong /oy/	102	oi	oil
OI Diphthong /oy/	115	oy	boy
OU Diphthong /ou/	27	ou	out
OU Diphthong	10,40,43	ow	owl
OO Long /ōō/ or /ü/	28, 114	oo	food
OO Long	14, 50	u	truth
OO Long	60	ew	new
OO Short /ŏŏ/ or /ù/	44, 114	oo	foot
OO Short	14, 28, 114		put
U Long /ū/		u	unite
U Short /ŭ/	7	u	up
U Short /ŭ/	51	o	oven
Schwa /ə/	51	o	idiom
Schwa /ə/	54, 105	a	canvas
Schwa /ə/	48	e	rebel

CONSONANTS

Sound Phoneme	Lesson Number	Spelled Grapheme	Example
B	30	b	boy
CH	46	ch	chair
D	6	d	dog
F	3	f	fan
F	83, 3	ph	phone
G	20, 124	g	go
H	14, 25	h	hot
J	55	j	just
J	85, 124.	g	gem
K	26	k	king
K	8, 26	c	can
K	8, 26, 37	ck	back
K	98	ch	chorus
L	15, 82	l	let
L	2, 15, 78	ll	ball
M	10	m	me
N	16	n	no
NG	38	ng	sing
P	17	p	pig
QU (kw)	57	qu	queen
R	18	r	red
S	11	s	so
S	35	c	city
SH	52	sh	show
SH	65	ti	action
T	5	t	to
TH(voiceless)	12, 29	th	thin
TH (voiced)	12	th	this
V	22	v	very
W	23	w	with
WH /hw/	31, 162	wh	white
X /eks/	66	ex	except
X /ks/	71	x	box
Y /y/	49	y	yes
Z	53	z	zero
Z	4	s	has
Silent	45, 68	gh	right
	43, 102	k	know
	7, 33, 76, 125	e	come
	24, 41		
	103	t	whistle
	23	w	write
	169	s	isle

Laguna Beach Educational Books 245 Grandview, Laguna Beach, California 92651

PHONICS INDEX (cont'd.)

Phonogram	Lesson Number	Phonogram	Lesson Number

PHONOGRAMS

Phonogram	Lesson Number	Phonogram	Lesson Number
A		ept	146
ace	117	en	8
ack	37	end	68
ad	6	ent	106
ail	81	(er)	24
ain	14	ess	62
ake	13	(est)	24
all	18	et	20
ame	88		
amp	75	**I**	
ane	88	ice	84
ano	75	ide	51
an	1	ift	104
ance	70	ight	31
and	26	ill	11
ane	44	ind	19
ap	39	ine	47
ape	12	ing	25, 67
ar	33	ink	76
ard	86	ip	36
are	55	ite	31, 113
ark	34		
ass	43	**O**	
ast	52	ock	15
at	5	old	38
ate	32	one	61
(aw)	29	ook	17
(ay)	16	(or)	64
		ore	72
E		ot	74
each	90	out	120
ead	69	(ow)	10
eak	54	own	40
eal	85		
ean	63	**U**	
(ed)	21	um	50
ear	27	un	30
eat	46	ung	101
ed	20	ut	7
eek	121		
eel	42		
eep	45		
eet	89		
ell	49		

Laguna Beach Educational Books 245 Grandview, Laguna Beach, California 92651

PHONICS CHARTS
Frequent Consonants - Phonics Chart 1

T	**N**	**R**
to take not at	not no and in	run red from our
top	nut	ring

M	**D**	**S**
me my some from	do day good and	some so this us
man	dog	saw

L	**C**	**P**
little like will girl	can come because second	put pretty up jump
letter	cat c = /k/ before a, o, u	pencil

B	**F**	**V**
but be about remember	for from if before	very visit give leave
book	fish	valentine

Laguna Beach Educational Books 245 Grandview, Laguna Beach, California 92651

PHONICS CHARTS
Short Vowels - Phonics Chart 2

A   apple

and
at
as

can
bad
man

E   elephant

end
egg
every

when
get
red

I   Indian

in
is
it

with
will
little

O   ostrich

on
off
ox

not
box
stop

U   umbrella

up
us
until

but
much
just

---

1. "e" at the end of a word

    The letter "e" is silent
    at the end of a word

    are   some
    one   like

    (only sometimes does it make the preceding
    vowel long - Final "E" Rule)

2. "y" at the end of a word containing
    another vowel sound like long "e"

    very   many
    any   pretty

Laguna Beach Educational Books 245 Grandview, Laguna Beach, California 92651

PHONICS CHARTS
Less Frequent Consonants- Phonics Chart 3

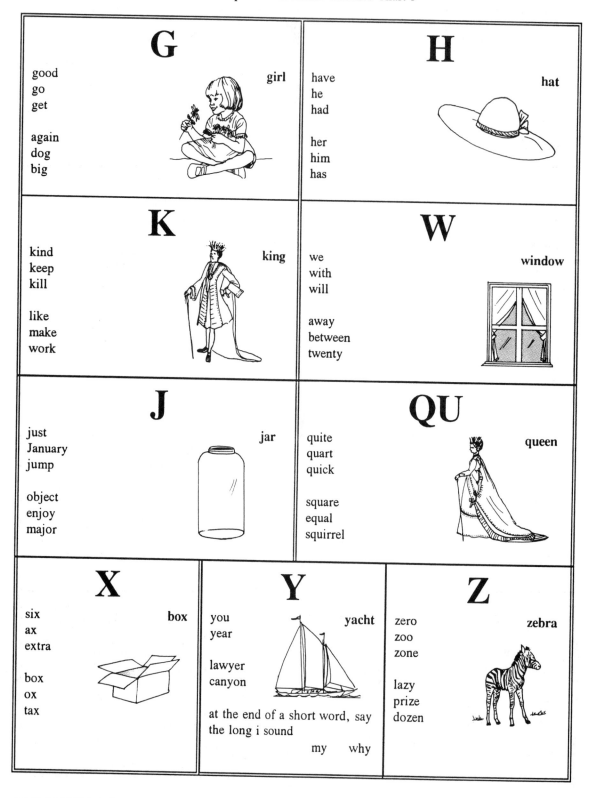

G

girl

good
go
get

again
dog
big

H

hat

have
he
had

her
him
has

K

king

kind
keep
kill

like
make
work

W

window

we
with
will

away
between
twenty

J

jar

just
January
jump

object
enjoy
major

QU

queen

quite
quart
quick

square
equal
squirrel

X

box

six
ax
extra

box
ox
tax

Y

yacht

you
year

lawyer
canyon

at the end of a short word, say the long i sound

my   why

Z

zebra

zero
zoo
zone

lazy
prize
dozen

Laguna Beach Educational Books 245 Grandview, Laguna Beach, California 92651

PHONICS CHARTS
Consonant Digraphs - Phonics Chart 4

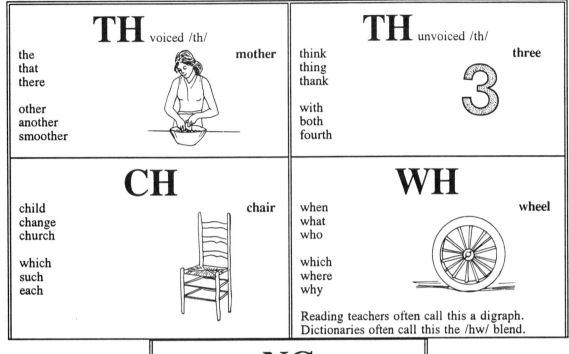

TH voiced /th/

the
that
there

other
another
smoother

mother

TH unvoiced /th/

think
thing
thank

with
both
fourth

three

CH

child
change
church

which
such
each

chair

WH

when
what
who

which
where
why

wheel

Reading teachers often call this a digraph.
Dictionaries often call this the /hw/ blend.

NG

swing sing string
rang   baking young

ring

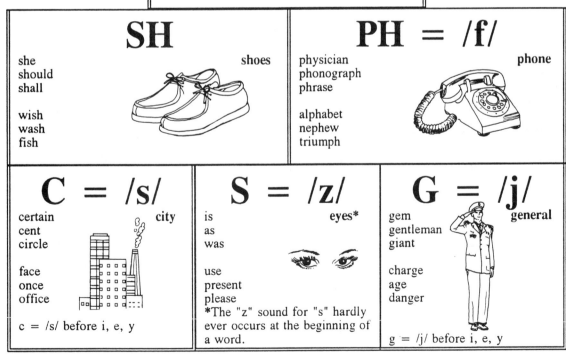

SH

she
should
shall

wish
wash
fish

shoes

PH = /f/

physician
phonograph
phrase

alphabet
nephew
triumph

phone

C = /s/

certain
cent
circle

face
once
office

city

c = /s/ before i, e, y

S = /z/

is
as
was

use
present
please
*The "z" sound for "s" hardly
ever occurs at the beginning of
a word.

eyes*

G = /j/

gem
gentleman
giant

charge
age
danger

general

g = /j/ before i, e, y

Laguna Beach Educational Books 245 Grandview, Laguna Beach, California 92651

PHONICS CHARTS
Long Vowels - Phonics Chart 5

Final "E" Rule: An "e" at the end of a word frequently makes the vowel long.

A	I
make	white
take	while
came	five
made	write
name	ride

O	U
home	use
those	produce
close	cube
hope	pure
note	tube

Exception: "e" - eve, here, Pete, Gene, these, scene
Exception: Long "u" - ew - new, dew, pew, slew, few, knew
  ue - cue, due, sue, hue

Open Syllable Rule: When a syllable ends in a vowel, that vowel frequently has the long sound.

A	E	I	O	U
table	we	I	so	duty
paper	be	idea	go	pupil
lady	he	pilot	no	music
baby	he	tiny	open	student

Vowel digraphs - there are only six common ones.

Long "e" EA EE	Long "a" AI AY	Long "o" OA OW
eat see	fail stay	coat own
year three	remain day	boat know
please seem	train gray	road show
easy sleep	aid clay	oak yellow

Laguna Beach Educational Books 245 Grandview, Laguna Beach, California 92651

PHONICS CHARTS
Schwa and Vowel Plus "r" - Phonics Chart 6

Schwa: The unaccented vowel in a word frequently has the sound of "a" in "ago". /ə/

A	E	O
about	happen	come
again	problem	other
away	bulletin	money
several	hundred	love

"er", "ir", and "ur" frequently all make the same sound.

ER	IR	UR
her	first	turn
were	girl	church
other	third	fur
after	sir	hurry

Plus sometimes "or" - honor, and sometimes "ar" - altar

"ar" has two sounds: "or" has a unique "o" sound /ô/

"ar" as in "far"   "ar" as in "vary"
/ä/   /"air"/

AR		OR
are	vary	for
far	Mary	or
start	care	before
hard	January	more

Like the Broad "o" sound

Laguna Beach Educational Books 245 Grandview, Laguna Beach, California 92651

PHONICS CHARTS
Diphthongs and Other Vowel Sounds - Phonics Chart 7

Broad "o" sound is made by "o", "al", "aw", and "au".

O	AL	AW	AU
on	all	saw	because
long	ball	law	auto
upon	also	awful	August
off	talk	lawn	haul

Exception:　"au" = /ă/ in laugh

Diphthongs make sliding sound from one vowel sound to another

OI	OY	OU	OW
"oi" and "oy" make the same sound.		"ou" and "ow" make the same sound.	
point	boy	out	how
voice	enjoy	about	down
coin	toy	our	brown
oil	royal	round	now

OO	OO	EA
/ü/ or /o͞o/ (spelled "oo", spelled "u")	/ù/ or /o͝o/ (spelled oo)	Short "ea" sound /ĕ/
Long Sound	Short Sound (spelled "u")	

OO		OO		EA
soon	June	good	put	ahead
school	rule	book	bush	heavy
too	blue	look	bull	ready
room	glue	took	full	bread

Laguna Beach Educational Books 245 Grandview, Laguna Beach, California 92651

PHONICS CHARTS
Initial Consonant Blends - Chart 8

Beginning Blends
These mainly fall into four families:
S family

ST	SP	SC	SK	SW	SM	SN
stand	sport	school	sky	swim	small	snake
state	space	scream	skate	sweep	smell	snow
stick	spot	scout	skin	swing	smart	snare
story	speed	scare	skirt	switch	smile	sneak
study	spend	screen	skip	sweet	smash	snap

R family

PR	TR	GR	BR	CR	DR	FR
pray	try	gray	bread	cry	dry	fry
price	tree	grade	broom	crazy	drink	from
press	trip	grow	brown	crew	dream	free
present	truck	grand	brake	cross	drum	front
pretty	trade	grass	bring	cream	drop	fruit

L family   TW family

PL	CL	BL	FL	SL	GL	TW
play	club	black	fly	slow	glad	twelve
plus	clown	blue	flag	slap	globe	twice
place	clay	blood	flat	sleep	glove	twin
plane	clear	blow	flood	slide	glass	twenty
plant	class	blame	flower	slip	glow	twist

Final Consonant Blends and Silent Consonants - Chart 9

Final blends

ND	NT	CT	NG	LD
and	ant	act	long	old
blond	bent	duct	sang	mild
grand	hunt	fact	king	told
band	can't	protect	finger	build
end	don't	subtract	young	wild

NC(e)	NK	RT	MP	PT	LT
once	ink	part	jump	kept	salt
since	think	smart	lamp	September	belt
dance	bank	heart	camp	slept	built
prince	trunk	hurt	bump	crept	melt
bounce	thank	art	stamp	swept	fault

Silent consonants

SILENT C BEFORE K	SILENT K BEFORE N	SILENT W BEFORE R	SILENT GH
back	know	write	high
luck	knife	wreck	right
rock	knee	wrist	taught
sick	knock	wrong	light
deck	knit	wrench	night

Exceptions: Almost any letter can be silent. Here are some examples:

g-gnaw	b-climb	e-come	p-pneumonia
h-rhyme	c-science	l-half	n-solemn

Laguna Beach Educational Books 245 Grandview, Laguna Beach, California 92651

SYLLABICATION RULES

The teaching of syllabication rules is somewhat controversial. Some say you should, and some say it is not worth the effort. Syllables sometimes are part of phonics lessons because syllabication affects vowel sounds (for example, the open syllable rule), and sometimes they are part of spelling or English lessons. There is no close agreement on various lists of syllabication rules, and some of the rules have plenty of exceptions. We are not urging you to teach them, but neither are we urging you to refrain from doing so.

There is a curious interaction between phonics and syllabication: some of the syllable rules work only if you know some phonics, and some phonics rules work only if you now the syllables. See Rules 1 and 2.

Rule 1. VCV   A consonant between two vowels tends to go with the second vowel unless the first vowel is accented and short.

                    Example: bro-ken, wag-on

Rule 2. VCCV   Divide two consonants between vowels unless they are a blend or digraph.

Rule 3. VCCCV   When there are three consonants between two vowels, divide between the blend or the digraph and the other consonant.

                    Example: an-gler

Rule 4. Affixes   Prefixes always form separate syllables (un-hap-py), and suffixes form separate syllables only in the following cases:

                    a. The suffix "-y" tends to pick up the preceding consonant.

                        Example: fligh-ty

                    b. The suffix "-ed" tends to form a separate syllable only when it follows a root that ends in "d" or "t".

                        Example: plant-ed

                    c. The suffix "-s" never forms a syllable except when it follows an "e".

                        Example: at-oms, cours-es

Rule 5. Compounds   Always divide compound words.

                    Example: black-bird

Rule 6. Final "le"   Final "le" picks up the preceding consonant to form a syllable.

                    Example: ta-ble

Laguna Beach Educational Books 245 Grandview, Laguna Beach, California 92651

SYLLABICATION RULES (cont'd.)

Rule 7. Vowel
            Clusters

Do not split common vowel clusters, such as:

a. "r"-controlled vowels (ar, er, ir, or, and ur).

    Example: ar-ti-cle

b. long vowel digraphs (ea, ee, ai, oa, and ow).

    Example: fea-ture

c. broad "o" clusters (au, aw, and al).

    Example: au-di-ence

d. diphthongs (oi, oy, ou, and ow).

    Example: thou-sand

e. double "o" digraph (oo).

    Example: moon

Rule 8. Vowel
            Problems

Every syllable must have one and only one vowel sound.

a. The letter "e" at the end of a word is silent.

    Example: come

    (If you want the long "e" /ē/ sound at the end of a two-syllable word, use a "y"; example: "funny".)

b. The letter "y" at the end or in the middle of a word operates as a vowel.

    Example: ver-y, cy-cle

    (Letter "y" at the end of a one-syllable word makes a long "i" /ī/; example: "fly", or the middle of a word "cycle".)

c. Two vowels together with separate sounds form separate syllables.

    Example: po-li-o

Laguna Beach Educational Books 245 Grandview, Laguna Beach, California 92651

TEST SHEET FOR LESSONS 1-20

Lesson No.: _____   Name: _____

Aa Bb Cc Dd Ee Ff Gg Hh Ii

Jj Kk Ll Mm Nn Oo Pp Qq

Rr Ss Tt Uu Vv Ww Xx Yy Zz

Spelling Words

1 _____   6 _____

2 _____   7 _____

3 _____   8 _____

4 _____   9 _____

5 _____   10 _____

Sentences

HANDWRITING CHARTS

Have you ever needed a handwriting chart for a special student and couldn't quickly locate one? The Zaner-Bloser manuscript and cursive alphabet charts are here to help you out in just such a situation. The D'Nealian alphabet is on the next page.

Zaner-Bloser Manuscript Alphabet

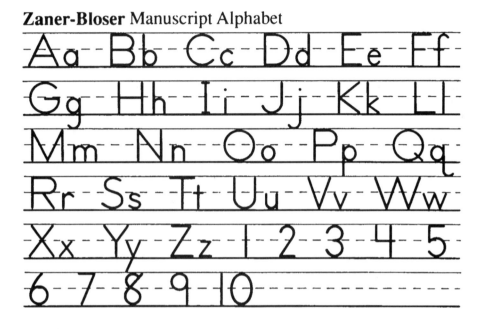

Zaner-Bloser Cursive Alphabet

Used with permission from *Handwriting: Basic Skills and Application.* Copyright © 1984 Zaner-Bloser, Inc., Columbus, Ohio.

Laguna Beach Educational Books 245 Grandview, Laguna Beach, California 92651

HANDWRITING CHARTS (cont'd)

D'Nealian™ Manuscript Alphabet

a b c d e f g h i
j k l m n o p q r
s t u v w x y z

A B C D E F G H I
J K L M N O P Q R
S T U V W X Y Z

D'Nealian™ Cursive Alphabet

a b c d e f g h i
j k l m n o p q r
s t u v w x y z

A B C D E F G H I
J K L M N O P Q R
S T U V W X Y Z

D'Nealian™ Numbers

0 1 2 3 4 5 6 7 8 9

Laguna Beach Educational Books 245 Grandview, Laguna Beach, California 92651

SPELLING PROGRESS CHART

Name

Lesson Number

WORDS / CORRECT																
20 / 100%																
19 / 95%																
18 / 90%																
17 / 85%																
16 / 80%																
15 / 75%																
14 / 70%																
13 / 65%																
12 / 60%																
11 / 55%																
10 / 50%																
9 / 45%																
8 / 40%																

Laguna Beach Educational Books 245 Grandview, Laguna Beach, California 92651

SUGGESTIONS TO PARENTS ON HELPING WITH SPELLING

1. Dictate the words for a trial spelling test. For example, the parent says a word, uses it in a sentence, and says the word again. The student writes the word from memory.

2. The student corrects his or her own trial test using the word list.

3. The parent checks to see if the correction is accurate.

4. The student should circle any errors or indicate omission of letters, then copy the word correctly, underlining the corrected letter.

5. Next the student should write any word missed several times from memory (without looking at the corrected word).

6. For a variation or additional practice, the parent can just say the word and the student says how to spell it orally.

7. Don't make the homework lessons too long. If the student is having trouble, do only part of the list at a time. Schools seldom devote over 15 or 20 minutes a day to spelling lessons. Homework lessons or trial tests should be shorter.

8. Reward the student with lots of verbal praise for words spelled correctly. It is difficult to learn to spell many words in the English language. Blame or ridicule doesn't help.

9. The mode of writing is not too important. For spelling, many students and teachers prefer manuscript handwriting (printing) because each letter can be seen in isolation. It is also fine for the student to type the words on a typewriter or computer wordprocessor during the test or for practice, especially if the student knows or is learning keyboarding (touch typing).

10. Spelling games like Scrabble® or Spelling Bees are helpful. Have a little fun with spelling.

11. Encourage writing. Have the student write letters, thank you notes, poems, stories, announcements, etc. Allow "invented" spelling while creating the written piece, then have the student proofread and correct with your help. Actually using some of the words from the spelling lists is helpful.

12. If you really want to be more helpful with home spelling lessons, encourage the student to keep a Personal Spelling List. This list is developed from words needed during writing, like grandmother's last name and city, or some special descriptive term. The Personal Spelling List might also contain words that presented special difficulty on spelling tests. The student can use the Personal Spelling List when writing later stories and the list can be used for trial spelling tests or games.

Laguna Beach Educational Books 245 Grandview, Laguna Beach, California 92651

MEMORY SUGGESTIONS

Memory aids, or mnemonics (ni-mon´-iks), are used in spelling for words that are exceptions and that do not follow phonics or more regular spelling patterns. Here are a few suggestions of different types of mnemonics. Feel free to make any of your own for troublesome words.

1. LITTLE WORDS IN BIG WORDS
>   (they often have some faint meaning link)
>   ex. principal - pal   hear - ear,   naturally - rally
>   cordial - dial   instead - tea   miscellaneous - cell

2. SIMILAR SPELLING PATTERN
>   (same phonemes and graphemes, sometimes with a meaning link)
>   ex. city - council   interfere - here   recess - necessary

3. ONE WORD OR TWO
>   ex. All right and all together are all separate (alright is non-standard).

4. SENTENCE OF EXCEPTION WORDS
>   ex. "ough" words - I thought I bought enough cough syrup to make it through this rough tough winter.
>
>   ex. "i before e" exceptions - Neither foreigner had a weird height either.

5. LETTER VISUALIZATIONS
>   ex. You need both "i's" for skiing.
>   ex. The last letter is curved in arc (not in ark).

6. ACRONYMS
>   (words made from first letters)
>   ex. arithmetic - A Rat In The House Might Eat The Ice Cream

7. EXAGGERATED PRONUNCIATION
>   (Distorted pronunciation makes the word more phonetic; good for some silent letters and schwa vowels.)
>   ex. Wed-nes-day   fav-or   of-ten   pen-cil

8. CLEVER LINKS
>   A shepherd herds sheep.
>   Miss Pell can't spell (double "s" for misspell).
>   There is no X (rating) for ecstasy.
>   There is a rat in separate.
>   You make a stake, but eat a steak.
>   Arrow rhymes with narrow.

If you would like to see 800 mnemonics for spelling words, get "Demon Mnemonics" by Sid Murray (Dell paperback).

Laguna Beach Educational Books 245 Grandview, Laguna Beach, California 92651

Franklin Pierce College Library

00035612

BIBLIOGRAPHY

Carroll, John B., Peter Davies and Barry Richman, <u>The American Heritage Word Frequency Book</u>, Houghton Mifflin Company, Boston, 1971.

Dean, John, <u>Games Make Spelling Fun</u>.   David S. Lake Publishers, Belmont, CA 1973.

Dewey, Godfrey, <u>Relative Frequency of English Spellings</u>. Teachers College Press, New York, 1970.

Donoghue, Mildred, <u>The Child and the English Language Arts</u>, Wm. C. Brown Publishers, Dubuque, Iowa, 1990.

Fry, Edward, "Picture Nouns for Reading and Vocabulary Improvement", <u>The Reading Teacher</u>, November 1987.

Hanna, Paul R., Jean S. Hanna, Richard E. Hodges and Erwin H. Rudorf, Jr., <u>Phoneme-Grapheme Correspondences as Cures to Spelling Improvement</u> OE 32008, U.S. Department of Health, Education and Welfare, Washington, DC, 1966.

Hanna, Paul R., Richard E. Hodges and Jean S. Hanna, <u>Spelling: Structure and Strategies</u>, Houghton Mifflin Company, Boston 1971.

Henderson, Edmund H., <u>Teaching Spelling</u>, Houghton Mifflin Company, Boston, 1985.

Hodges, Richard E., <u>Learning to Spell: Theory and Research Into Practice</u>, National Council of Teachers of English, Urbana, IL, 1981.

Horne, E., "The Curriculum for the Gifted", <u>Twenty Third Yearbook of the National Society for the Study of Education</u>, Part 1, 1924.

Sakiey, Elizabeth and Edward Fry, <u>3000 Instant Words</u>, Jamestown Publishers, Providence, RI, 1984.

Shaw, Harry, <u>Spell It Right!</u>, Harper and Row, New York, NY, 1986.

Thorndike, Edward L. and Irving Lorge, <u>The Teachers Word Book of 30,000 Words</u>, Teachers College Press, New York, NY, 1944.

Webster, Noah, <u>The Elementary Spelling Book</u>, American Book Company, New York, NY, 1857 & 1908.

_____, <u>Questions Asked Most Frequently About Spelling and Answers According to Spelling Research</u>, McDougal, Littel and Company, Evanston, IL, 1989.